ISSUES FOR THE SEVENTIES

ENVIRONMENTAL QUALITY

ISSUES FOR THE SEVENTIES

ENVIRONMENTAL
QUALITY

EDITED BY

NORMAN SHEFFE, B.A., A.M. (Harvard)

Consultant for the Social Sciences
Lincoln County Board of Education
St. Catharines, Ontario

McGRAW-HILL
Company of Canada Limited

Toronto   Montreal   New York   London   Sydney
Mexico   Johannesburg   Panama   Düsseldorf   Singapore
Rio de Janeiro   Kuala Lumpur   New Delhi

ISSUES FOR THE SEVENTIES

ENVIRONMENTAL QUALITY

ISBN   0-07-092859-2

12345678910   MB71   0987654321

Printed and bound in Canada

CONTENTS

ACKNOWLEDGEMENTS

The cover photographs are courtesy of *The St. Catharines Standard*, as well as the photographs on pages 24 and 83.

Photographs on pages 6 and 62 are by John McTaggart of the *St. Catharines Standard*.

The photograph on page 116 is by Bev Christensen of the *St. Catharines Standard*.

The photograph on page 96 is from the NFB. Photographs on pages 19 and 43 are by Chris Lund of the NFB.

The photograph on page 105 is by Gar Lumney of the NFB.

The illustration on page 68 is courtesy of the Ford Motor Company.

INTRODUCTION

Ecology

      . . . environmental quality

           . . . conservation

               . . . atmospheric contamination

                  . . . earth day

These words have an ominous ring! Our common vocabulary has been invaded by new and strange-sounding words and terms. We are increasingly made aware by the mass media that all is not right with our environment. In nearly every issue of popular newspapers and magazines, stories appear featuring details of one more oil spill, smoke menace, pesticide, litter, or noise pollution endangering our lives.

Popular entertainers have quickly adapted their jokes and wisecracks to take advantage of topical interest in the subject. Songs (sometimes wryly sick like those of Tom Lehrer) have mourned over the fate towards which we seem to be heading. Shrewd business enterprises — merchants of air purifiers, anti-smog devices, organically grown foods — are only a few of the more obvious spin-offs of the pollution scare. More nonphosphate detergents, new types of water purifiers, as well as some highly sophisticated industrial equipment for waste-producing manufacturers can be looked for in the immediate future. The scope of the pollution problem is such that an *anti-pollution industry* is springing up to take advantage of the nervous public interest in environmental products.

The economics of pollution are a matter of grave concern for every citizen — not only the costs which accrue from the misuse of our surroundings, but also the costs of prevention and correction. Inevitably, the scope of the issue is economic, social and ethical in nature, and of course, technical as well. The citizen must be prepared to examine the implications of pollution, considering not only the origin of the problem but also the effects of reform programs. Scientists can prepare procedure and devices for dealing with specific problems, but the citizen, often working through elected representatives, must make the decisions involving the acceptance or rejection of one kind of action or another — and he must make the decisions after balancing the costs involved against the survival of man and life on earth.

For example, if a factory is pouring its untreated waste products into a local stream or lake, thus upsetting the natural balance of life of the water, the people both near and far have a vested interest in the situation. Does the company have a property right to use the land it owns in any manner it wishes? Does the owner of adjacent property have rights which require protection? May public waters be freely used by an industry? If an industry has been in the habit of using public water over a long period of time without protest from the citizenry, has a right to continue using those waters been established by habitual usage? If citizens are concerned about such practices, how can they persuade the polluter to alter his ways? If a new procedure is to be introduced to avoid polluting, who must bear the burden of the cost? The owners? The public at large (by government assistance to industry)? The consumer through higher prices for the products manufactured? Or a combination of these groups?

One industrialist has bluntly said that "if industry pollutes, then industry must pay the bill for cleaning up the mess." But who, in reality, will cover that bill — the owner, or shareholder, paying for the cleanup out of profits — or the consumer? Are cleanup costs a necessary element of production costs?

Supposing the factory owner considers cleanup costs are greater than they are worth to him; can he be forced to accept them? If he decides that he would be better off closing his business rather than changing his disposal system, what effect will this have on the local economy? May he use the threat of taking such action to avoid cleaning up? How are we to prepare ourselves to make the necessary decisions?

The current interest in pollution problems, then, must be seen as a public recognition of the greater question — what kind of life should man be leading on earth? The threat to the entire human race has been with us since the first atomic bomb was dropped; we are now trying to grapple with other types of threats almost as horrifying.

Why pollution? People pollute by demanding goods and services in greater numbers than ever before — production breeds waste. New technologies create new waste problems — sometimes in the form of waste radioactive materials whose potential cannot be accurately determined. The population explosion brings with it demands for more food, drinking water, space to live, work to perform, goods to consume, and services to use. The chain of demands has side effects in the form of wastes left over from human consumption, technical processes, and the movement of goods and people from one place to another.

The polluter is often unconscious of the fact that he is creating environmental problems — the automobile driver, the cigarette smoker, the user of electric power are all adding to the noxious fumes building up in our atmosphere. The housewife doing the weekly wash with a high-phosphate detergent is not deliberately and calculatingly killing Lake Erie, nor is the pleasure-boat enthusiast who pumps his bilge into the crystal clear water. Thoughtless use of our resources has made everyone responsible.

There are a few encouraging signs. In several of the articles that follow are statements by enlightened industrialists which give us some reason to be optimistic. Nevertheless, there is still a feeling that deeds, not words, are needed.

Among the most pressing problems of our time, few appear to be more difficult to solve and yet so frightening in potential danger as the one involving

... earth day

    ... atmospheric contamination

        ... environmental quality

            ... ecology and

                ... pollution

                  N.S.

Part 1

Life is sustained on earth by a precarious balance of all the elements needed for survival. Imbalances, when they occur, have far-reaching effects which interfere with patterns of survival of plants, animals and human societies. Theorists have suggested that the fall of the Roman Empire might have been partially caused by farming methods which allowed the topsoil to gradually erode; thus the once-fertile areas of the eastern Mediterranean were changed into barren stretches within a few centuries. A land of milk and honey became a vast wasteland.

Man's record as far as his management of the environment is concerned has not been particularly good. But is it possible to turn back the clock to find out where we went wrong and to begin anew? There's not much time left for us to do this. Required are not only the limited hours at our disposal, but most important, a new ethic to guide us on our way.

TESTIMONY OF J. G. HARRAR

Hearings on the environmental quality Education Act (H.R. 14753) before the house select subcommittee on education

My name is J. George Harrar and I am president of The Rockfeller Foundation. My professional education and experience have been principally in the area of science — in particular, in biology.

The legislation — bill H.R. 14753 — being deliberated here today would in my opinion contribute significantly toward a better understanding of our ecological crisis and toward educating the public as to the importance of environmental responsibility.

Environmental damage has been going on for years, but it is only recently that its rate has become so accelerated and its effects so widespread as to create a general concern and growing awareness that we are face to face with an ecological crisis. More and more people now recognize the need for immediate measures to arrest the palpable threat to the quality of life and realize that there is no single-formula solution to the problem. Numerous individuals and groups in both public and private life are currently attempting, each in their own way and in their own specialized fields, to cope with, or at least to push back to some degree, the impending crisis. Municipal authorities, scientists, doctors, technicians, state and federal legislators, city planners, university faculties and students, philanthropists, and corporations are increasingly involved in finding ways to prevent the further impairment of our environment, to slow down its rate of deterioration, or to repair the damage done thus far.

I, and I am sure many others, are particularly gratified by those sections of the proposed "Environmental Quality Education Act" that seek to establish and encourage education and information programs that will lead to a better understanding on the part of everyone — teachers, students, and other citizens — of man's place and responsibility within that totally interrelated scheme of things that we call nature. We have come to realize all too slowly that man despite his extraordinary technological triumphs is, and always will be, dependent on his physical environment — the earth, air, and water that is his home.

At this critical juncture, when we are finally coming to realize the hazards and dangers of our situation, it would be well for man to question the validity of his attitudes toward nature and to consider seriously the desirability and wisdom of formulating a new ethic for dealing with his natural environment

Reprinted by permission of the author, Dr. J. G. Harrar.

which would transcend most of the values we have traditionally held concerning our world.

The Bible tells us that God gave man dominion over all the earth and over every living creature on it. Man has misinterpreted this injunction as a license to exploit rather than a conferral of responsibility. In the last analysis, man does indeed have dominion over all the earth, but this puts him under grave obligations. Morally, no society has the right to over-utilize the world's resources for its own contemporary and selfish interests. Man must understand biological systems and conduct his affairs in such ways as to improve the quality of life rather than degrade it through wanton exploitation.

It is admirable and public-spirited to be deeply committed to the well-being of the present generation of human beings who here and now inhabit the earth, and hopefully this attitude will grow and continue. It is even more commendable for men living today to become increasingly concerned about the future of their children and their children's children in the face of a worsening environment. But the new ethic of ecological responsibility must extend far beyond even this highly humanitarian concern. It must embody the highest responsibility of all — the ultimate responsibility for the total natural environment, the biosphere, and life itself — not human life only, but *all life,* in its varied and diverse forms.

The first principle of the new ethic would be that man must control his own fertility. Whether we are concerned primarily with the present population of the world, with future generations, with man's survival as a species, or with preserving the stability of the entire biosphere, it is absolutely imperative that the human birth rate be curtailed. Man's superior intelligence and his belief in the intrinsic worth of each human being do not entitle him to assume that the natural environment should be given over to the production and maintenance of his own kind. Instead, it would be incumbent upon him, as the only species capable of making moral decisions, to live up to his total responsibilities and move toward a goal of zero rate of population increase.

The new ethic would also reject the premise that technology alone can provide answers to all or most of our environmental problems. It is true that technology has been a major and constructive force in the development of our society, and is using its inventiveness today to provide new methods of cleaning up after itself, of controlling pollution at its source, and of re-using the residuals being produced by our present industrial system. But technology does have its limitations. Advanced technology has a tendency to create the need for even more technology and often merely substitutes one kind of pollution for another.

It is easy to blame technology for many of our environmental ills, but it must be remembered that technological advances are often in direct response to public demand. The entire society has the responsibility of recognizing what we are doing to our environment and of making individual and collective efforts to reverse the negative effects of certain forms of technology. We are prone to overvalue the production of nonessential material goods which rapidly become obsolescent and are eventually consigned to the already tremendous body of accumulated waste that is piling up around us. We must, of necessity, adopt self-imposed restraints by which the individual voluntarily refrains from contributing further to our ecological imbalance and is ever conscious of the need to conserve and not to destroy. Only when increasing numbers of individuals, groups, and communities recognize and accept their responsibilities and take organized action can improvement occur. Today, in this country, we have more than 200 million people, all contributing in some measure to the degradation of their environment. When these individuals can be persuaded to embrace the new ethic, to become "conservers" in the best sense of the word, a major victory will have been won.

The third principle of the ethic of responsibility for the environment is that we, in the more advanced nations at least, should put considerably less emphasis on that form of economic growth that simply multiplies production and consumption of material goods. We dwell in a finite world where many changes and processes are irreversible. Our resources are not limitless, and when those that are nonrenewable are consumed or transformed, they can never be replenished. Our present resources should be carefully husbanded and conserved. With stabilized populations, more attention and resources could and should be devoted to services and to those areas of life that enrich the quality of human existence: cultural activities, the arts, literature, intellectual and scientific pursuits, aesthetic improvements, and human relationships.

A final basic principle is that man should consider the equilibrium of the natural environment before initiating any actions that would disturb existing ecosystems. Modern technology, urban expansion, and rapid industrialization have drastically altered the ecological balance in many localities, extinguishing certain plant life and animal species. Complex genetic material, once destroyed, cannot be recreated in a laboratory. Not only will the natural environment be altered and impoverished; it will become a much less varied, interesting, and desirable place for man to live.

The proposed legislation, if enacted, could, in my opinion, be of great value in bringing Americans of all ages and all educational levels to a recognition of the urgency of the problem and to an understanding of their responsibilities in maintaining and enhancing environmental quality.

NATURE UNDER ATTACK

Barry Commoner

*Barry Commoner, Chairman of the De-
partment of Botany and Director of the
Center for the Biology of Natural Systems
at Washington University, St. Louis, is a
graduate of Columbia College, 1937. His
book* Science and Survival, *published by
Viking Press in 1966, and his many activities promoting public information about
science reflect a deep interest in the inter-
action between science and social problems.*

The proliferation of human beings on
the surface of this planet is proof of the
remarkable suitability of the terrestrial
environment as a place for human life.
But the fitness of the environment is
not an immutable feature of the earth,
having been developed by gradual
changes in the nature of the planet's
skin. Living things have themselves
been crucial agents of these transformations, converting the earth's
rocks into soil, releasing oxygen from
its water, transforming carbon dioxide
into accumulated fossil fuels, modulat-
ing temperature and tempering the
rush of waters on the land. And in the
course of these transformations, the
living things that populated the surface
of the earth have, with the beautiful
precision that is a mark of life, themselves become closely adapted to the
environment they have helped to
create. As a result, the environment in
which we live is itself part of a vast
web of life, and like everything associated with life is internally complex,
and stable, not in a static sense, but
by virtue of the intricate play of internal interactions.

On a small scale, the dependence of
environmental stability on the nice
balance of multiple biological processes is self-evident. A hillside denuded
of vegetation by fire and thus lacking
protection against the erosion of heavy
rains previously afforded by the canopy
of leaves and the mat of roots can
quickly shed its soil and lose its cap-
ability to support plants and harbor
animals. And on this scale, the threat
of thoughtless human interventions is
equally self-evident; we have long
since learned that brutal lumbering or
greedy exploitation of the soil can
permanently alter the life-supporting
properties of a forest or a once-fertile
plain. On this scale, too, we know, from
the wastelands that surround our
smelters, or from the disappearance of
shellfish in a polluted estuary, that
human ingenuity is rapidly creating
new and more devastating hazards to
the stability of the environment. We
also know of numerous specific risks to
particular living components of the
biosphere — that DDT threatens to
wipe out the bird's of prey; that industrial wastes kill off a river's game fish;
that sewage renders a beach unusable.

Such small-scale and specific assaults
on the living environment illuminate

Reprinted from the *Columbia Forum*, Spring 1968, Volume XI, Number 1. Copyright 1968 by
The Trustees of Columbia University in the City of New York. By permission of Barry Commoner.

the basic principles that govern the impact of human intrusions on the environment: (1) Because of the complex network of interactions in the environment an intrusion in one place may exert its main effect in a distant locale. Massive nuclear weapons have often been exploded on isolated Pacific Islands. But, because of the peculiarities of the lichen-caribou-man food chain on which they depend, it has been the Eskimos and Lapps living in the Arctic Circle that are most seriously affected by worldwide fallout generated by these blasts. (2) Food chains and nutritive metabolism constitute a kind of biological amplifier which can enormously intensify an originally weak intrusion on the environment. Thus, DDT sprayed at a low concentration accumulates in plankton, is further concentrated in the fish that feed on plankton, ultimately reaching a peak concentration in the birds that prey on fish. In this way DDT becomes several-hundredfold concentrated in the osprey and the eagle, which fall accidental prey to our war on insects. (3) Like any other system comprised of complex feedback cycles, an ecosystem tends to oscillate (witness the well-known interacting cycles of wolf and rabbit populations). And like other oscillating processes, an ecosystem can be driven into self-accelerating changes, and to ultimate collapse, by over-stressing at a particularly vulnerable point. Thus over-fertilization of surface waters can so accelerate the growth of algae as to deplete the oxygen content (in the dark hours) so that the algae themselves die and pollute the water. These principles tell us what is required for the stability of the environment in which we live and for its continued suitability as a place for human life. The system must accommodate itself to the stresses placed upon it in such a way as to maintain the internal processes which account for its stability.

How has the living environment been faring under these stresses? Where has the system managed to accommodate itself and achieve a new, if different, but stable balanced state? What stresses are still in the process of altering the environmental system, and what is the forecast of a new stable equilibrium? Are the changes accelerating? Is there a danger of stressing the system as a whole to the point of collapse?

The most direct human contact with the environment is mediated by the air, for a massive amount of this substance is continuously brought into intimate contact with internal metabolism through the lungs. Natural air contains only oxygen, nitrogen, water vapor, carbon dioxide, rare gases, some volatile biological products, and occasional dust. But the air that most of us breathe, especially in the cities, now contains as well: increasing amounts of oxides of nitrogen and sulfur, various kinds of dust and soot, particles of rubber and asbestos, carbon monoxide, and a wide array of poorly identified organic componds.

Ten years ago automotive smog was a problem found almost entirely in Los Angeles, and sulfur dioxide hazards were apparent only in isolated industrial regions such as Donora, Pennsylvania. Now, New York City experiences acute episodes involving both automotive smog and sulfur dioxide, I know from personal observations that the incidence and extent of smog pollution in St. Louis has increased sharply in the last 20 years. Denver, once famed for its clear mountain air, is now subject to smog. Clearly this stress on the environment is worsening.

And while the general level of air pollution is rising there is reason to believe that the incidence of disease associated with it will rise more rapidly than the pollutant concentrations themselves. Consider, for example, the problem of lung cancer arising from chemicals such as benzopyrene which are found in the polluted city air. Airborne organic carcinogens such as benzopyrene are capable of inducing lung cancer because of their influence on cells that line the air passages of the lungs. Laboratory studies show that the degree of the carcinogenic hazard rises with the concentration of carcinogen to which the cells are exposed and with the duration of contact between the carcinogen and the susceptible cells. There are protective mechanisms in the lung that tend to limit exposure to materials drawn in from the air, and any additional air pollutant that inhibits these mechanisms will influence the effect of a given concentration of the air-borne carcinogen. For example, sulfur dioxide tends to paralyze the ciliated cells of the lung air passages and thereby cut down the self-protective cleansing process in the lung. For this reason sulfur dioxide will extend the time of contact between a carcinogen such as benzopyrene and the lung. In this situation the risk of carcinogenesis must be measured by the *product*; benzopyrene concentration multiplied by sulfur dioxide concentration. If the concentrations of both pollutants double, we must expect that the risk of carcinogenesis may rise by as much as a factor of four.

Unfortunately, we do not yet have sufficient public health data to generalize about the quantitative relations between the level of air pollution and the medical effects associated with it. However, in the relatively sparse data available there is already some evidence that the health effects associated with pollution may be rising faster than the over-all level of pollution itself.

Thus, although the concentration of organic air pollutants (a class that includes carcinogens such as benzopyrene) increases more or less proportionally with city size, the incidence of cancer in cities of different sizes seems to rise with city size not linearly but exponentially. Obviously there are other factors involved in this problem, but the present information should certainly warn us that the health effects from air pollution may worsen faster than the pollution level itself — a result expected from the multiplicative effects of air pollutants.

The dependence of human society on large supplies of fresh water is deep and pervasive. In addition to its direct biological necessity to man, water is essential in vast amounts for almost every industrial process. In natural lakes and rivers, animal organic wastes are degraded by the action of bacteria of decay which convert them into inorganic substances: carbon dioxide, nitrates, and phosphates. In turn these substances nourish plants, which provide food for the animals. In sunlight, plants also add to the oxygen content of the water and so support animals and the bacteria of decay. All this makes up a tightly woven cycle of mutually dependent events, which in nature maintains the clarity and purity of the water and sustains its population of animals, plants, and micro-organisms.

We use this natural self-purifying system to control urban wastes. Sewage treatment plants add considerable amounts of organic substances to the lakes and rivers that receive their outflow, although the increment is reduced by the treatment. If all goes well the biological cycle assimilates the added organic materials, and, maintaining its balance, keeps the water pure. But such a complex cyclical system, with its important feedback loops, cannot indefinitely remain balanced in the face of a steadily increasing organic load. Sufficiently stressed it becomes vulnerable at certain critical points. For example, the bacteria that act on organic wastes must have oxygen, which is consumed as the waste is destroyed. If the waste load becomes too high, the oxygen content of the water falls to zero, the bacteria die, the biological cycle breaks down, the purification process collapses, and the water becomes foul.

The water pollution problem has become urgent chiefly because we are allowing the organic content of surface waters to approach the breaking point. The first large-scale warning is the death of Lake Erie, where, as a result of the rapid accumulation of wastes, most of the central portion of the lake has gone to zero oxygen. The lake's life-cycle has been forced out of balance and what was, for tens of thousands of years, a beautifully clear and productive inland sea in a decade has become a rank, muddy sink.

Even universal use of present waste disposal technology will not get us out of trouble, for the treatment systems themselves elevate the nitrate and phosphate content of the receiving waters. These substances are always present in natural waters — but in amounts far less than those generated by the huge waste load imposed on them by man. And at such abnormally high levels, nitrate and phosphate become a new hazard to the biological balance. These concentrated nutrients may induce a huge growth of algae — an algae "bloom." Such an enormously dense population tends to die off with equal suddenness, again overloading the water with organic debris, and disrupting the natural cycle. And nitrate, if sufficiently concentrated, may be toxic to man. About 8-9 parts per million of nitrate in an infant's drinking

water may interfere with hemoglobin function; in a number of areas of the United States, water supplies have reached nitrate levels of 3 parts per million. In some places, physicians have been forced to replace tap water in infant diets.

In 1900 the total amount of nitrogen discharged to U.S. streams by municipal sewage was about 200 million pounds per year. Rising since then at an accelerating rate, the amount reached 1,200 million pounds per year in 1963 and is expected to reach about 2,000 million pounds per year by 2000. From 1900 to 1940 phosphate discharged into U.S. streams by municipal sewage rose from about 10 million pounds (as phosphorus) per year to about 30 million pounds per year. But, thereafter, the rate of increase accelerated so rapidly that in 1963 the annual phosphorus burden was 250 million pounds and is expected to double again by 2000. The total oxygen demand on surface waters for degradation of organic materials in municipal sewage more than doubled between 1900 and 1960. The increase has been held in check by the production of new sewage treatment plants, but these plants do not, of course, reduce the burden of inorganic residues, such as nitrate, imposed on surface water.

Clearly our aqueous environment is being subjected to an accelerating stress, which will become so severe in the next few decades as to threaten to collapse the self-purifying biological system on which we rely for usable water.

Finally we can look at the status of the nation's soil. The soil is, of course, the basis for the initial production of nearly all of our food resources, and many industrial raw materials as well. The soil is a vastly complex ecosystem, its fundamental capabilities for supporting plant life being the resultant of an intricate balance among a wide variety of micro-organisms, animals, and plants, acting on a long-established physical substrate.

The complicated biology of the soil ties the fate of the city and industrial plant to the farm. Crop plants convert nitrates and other plant nutrients to protein. In nature, let us say a plant growing in a wood or meadow, nitrate reaches the soil chiefly as the product of bacterial decay of organic wastes — manure and the bodies of animals and plants. The natural concentration of nitrate in the soil water is very low and the roots need to work to pull it into the plant. For this work the plant must expend energy which is released by biological oxidation processes in the roots. These processes require oxygen, which can reach the roots only if the soil is sufficiency porous. Soil porosity is governed by its physical structure; in particular a high level of organic nitrogen, in the form of humans, is required to maintain a porous soil structure. Thus, soil porosity, therefore its oxygen content, and hence the efficiency of nutrient absorption, is closely related to the organic nitrogen content of the soil.

When the United States was settled, the soil system was in this natural condition; the soil cycle was in balance maintaining its nitrogen reserve in the stable organic form. Only small amounts of inorganic salts drained off into the rivers which remained clear and unburdened with pollutants. As the continent was settled, the natural soil system was taken over for agricultural purposes. Plants were grown on the soil in amounts much greater than they would sustain in nature. The organic store of nutrients was gradually depleted and crop yields declined year by year. With virgin lands always available, farmers moved westward, re-

peating the process of skimming from the soil the most available nutrient and leaving it when its productivity fell below a certain point, which made westward migration more attractive. This process, of course, came to an end about 1900 and from then on as crop production became intensified to meet the demands of a growing population, more and more of the original store of organic nutrients was withdrawn from the soil in the form of crops. In the Midwest the organic content of soil has declined about 50 percent in the last 100 years. As a result, the productivity of the soil has declined.

For a time nutrients were returned to the soil by use of animal manures and imported fertilizers, especially guano. With the growth of the chemical industry it became possible to produce much cheaper inorganic nutrients as fertilizer. The heavy use of inorganic fertilizer began especially in the cotton and tobacco land of the South. Here, because of high climatic temperatures which stimulates the breakdown of the organic stores of the soil, the soil was particularly impoverished and spectacular gains in yields could be obtained from inorganic fertilizers. In the 1940s there began a striking increase all over the nation in the use of inorganic fertilizers. The use of inorganic nitrogen fertilizer has increased about sevenfold in the last 25 years.

The result has been a massive stress of the soil ecosystem by the addition to it of huge and increasing quantities of nitrogen, phosphorus, potassium, and other plant nutrients. During heavy rains there is a natural tendency for the added inorganic fertilizer to wash out of the soil into rivers, especially in the case of nitrates. The available data show that under most field conditions an appreciable part of the added nitrogen fertilizer fails to enter the crop and instead leaves the soil in one of two forms. Part of this lost nitrogen, probably of the order of from 10 to 25 percent of the total fertilizer placed on the soil, drains out of the soil into rivers and lakes, the amount varying greatly with local soil conditions. Another part of the added nitrogen (perhaps 5 to 10 percent) leaves the soil because the excess nitrate and low soil oxygen content tend to stimulate bacterial formation of volatile forms of nitrogen (nitrogen oxides and ammonia). This volatilized nitrogen is caught up in rain and is washed down again to the ground, and eventually into rivers and lakes where it adds to the inorganic nitrogen already present. Investigators have been continually surprised of late to find large amounts of nitrogen in rainfall. For example, studies in Wisconsin show that rainfall now often contains as much as one part per million of nitrogen. In contrast earlier studies showed nitrogen content of rain to be of the order of .2 of one part per million.

The seriousness of the agricultural contribution to water pollution is evident from the following data: In 1964 municipal sewage in the United States contributed a total of about 1,200 million pounds of nitrogen to surface waters, ultimately in the form of nitrate. In that same year agriculture added about 8,000 million pounds of nitrogen to the soil in the form of inorganic fertilizers. If only 15 percent of this fertilizer leached out of the soil into surface waters — a percentage often observed in field experiments — the amount of nitrogen imposed on surface waters would be equivalent to the amount originating in municipal sewage. And, it should be added, there is no sign that the increasing use of inorganic fertilizer will slacken in the next decade.

Thus, universal use of secondary treatment methods for urban sewage, and corresponding control of industrial organic wastes, will nevertheless burden surface waters with large amounts of the inorganic residues of treatment, especially nitrate. At the same time, nitrate leaching from fertilized farmland will probably double this burden, leading to massive overgrowths of algae which, on their death, cause a new cycle of organic pollution. By means of advanced treatment methods, it would be possible to remove inorganic nutrients from the effluent of municipal and industrial waste systems, but a corresponding control of nutrients from farmland runoff would require treatment of the total mass of surface water — a forbidding task. We might undertake a huge program of controlling sewage and industrial waste only to find that rivers and lakes were dying from overfeeding by farmland fertilizer runoff.

In large part, agricultural production has increased in the United States in order to sustain the increasing population in this country and elsewhere and also to support a rising U.S. per capita consumption. In order to accomplish this increased food production we have massively stressed the nitrogen cycle in the soil by the introduction of inorganic fertilizer and this process, in turn, may stress to the breaking point the self-purifying aqueous systems upon which we depend for our urban waste disposal. This process may well turn out to be the most immediate mechanism whereby increasing population exerts a negative feedback on the quality of the environmental system sustaining it.

We have only begun to perceive the vast economic, social, and political conflicts that are being generated by the crisis in the environment. The nation is already in the throes of a tangled struggle with the problem of urban air pollution. This involves pervasive issues in transportation, power production, and basic urban design, which add enormously to the complex situation in the ecosystem itself. If coal-burning power plants contaminate the air with sulfur dioxide, shall we replace them with apparently "clean" nuclear reactors — and run the risks of radioactive contamination from waste-handling and the small but catastrophic risks of an accident in a highly populated area? If, in order to cure the smog problem we need to replace gasoline-burning vehicles with electric ones, how can the power industry and the petroleum industry accommodate this massive change?

Subtle, but vital, interactions operate in this area. For example, the New York City power industry is preparing to build a proposed water-storage generating plant on the Hudson River at Storm King Mountain in order to use excess nighttime generating capacity to store energy for daytime use. But if New York's vehicles are to be driven by electric motors, their batteries will need to be charged at night, and this will surely wipe out the nighttime excess in generating capacity that is the basis for the Storm King proposal.

Similar conflicts surround most of our environmental problems, but the ones that we have yet to confront will be vastly more serious. The economic and political impact of farm productivity on the nation is, of course, massive and pervasive. The present financial status of American agriculture is heavily based on the massive use of inorganic fertilizer. Since 1950 the cost to the American farmer of the land, machinery, and labor that he uses has increased about 80, 40, and 60 percent respectively. In contrast, the cost of fertilizer has *dropped* about 20 percent.

The values of land, machinery, and labor inputs into farming have all declined in that period; in contrast, the input value of fertilizer has increased more than 80 percent. Clearly any effort to limit the use of inorganic fertilizer on U.S. farms — and I can foresee no other way of ensuring the integrity of our waste disposal systems — will set off a series of explosive economic and political problems.

The crisis in the environment reveals a potentially fatal flaw in the social use of modern science and technology. We have developed an enormous competence to intervene in the natural world: we can release fearful nuclear explosions, spray insecticides over the countryside, and produce millions of automobiles. But at the same time we are unable to predict the full biological consequences of nuclear war or to avoid risks to our livelihood and health from the side effects of the insecticides or from the smog that our autos produce. In the eager search for the benefits of modern science and technology we have blundered into the accompanying hazards before we were aware of them.

In 1956 the government thought there was no harm associated with nuclear tests; but we now know from the thyroid nodules in Utah children that this was a tragic mistake. We exploded the bombs *before* we had the scientific knowledge to understand the biological and medical consequence.

We produced power plants and automobiles which envelop our cities in smog — before we understood its harmful effects on health. We learned how to synthesize and use new insecticides — before we learned that they also kill birds and might be harmful to people. We produced detergents and put billions of pounds on the market — before we realized that they would make water supplies foam and should be taken off the market. We are ready to conduct a nuclear war — even though we do not know whether the effect of the vast catastrophe on life, on soil, and the weather will destroy our civilization.

Despite their complicated scientific background, the issues generated by environmental pollution do not lie in the domain of science. No scientific evaluation can determine how to share the inevitable costs of controlling water pollution among cities, industries, and farms. Scientific method cannot determine whether it is better to suffer the hazards of smog, or to undertake the huge economic cost of reorganizing urban transportation. No scientific principle can tell us how to make the choice between the prosperity of the farm and the welfare of the city. These are social and political issues and can only be resolved by social and political processes.

What can be done? Sometimes it is suggested that since scientists and engineers have made the bombs, insecticides, and autos, they ought to be responsible for deciding how to deal with the resultant hazards. But this would deprive everyone else of the right of conscience and the political rights of citizenship. This approach would also force us to rely on the moral and political wisdom of scientists and engineers, and there is no evidence that I know of that suggests they are better endowed in this respect than other people.

There is an alternative, which is feasible though difficult. I believe that citizens can continue to rely on their own collective judgment about the issues of environmental conservation — if they take steps to inform themselves. The nuclear test-ban treaty is a good example of how this can be done. It seems clear that one of the important reasons this treaty was approved by a vote of the Senate is that the Senators were informed by their constituents of their opposition to the radioactive poisoning of our foods by fallout. Where did the letter writers get the necessary facts? Largely from public education by many scientists who believe that these issues ought to be decided by public judgment.

Out of an original concern with fallout and nuclear war we have developed a new "information movement" among academic scientists, designed to educate the public about the scientific and technological facts relevant to the major issues of the day. This is the alliance between the scientist and the citizen, which Margaret Mead has called "a new social invention." On this alliance depends the hope that the morality of man can, at last, turn the enormous new power that science has given us from the path of catastrophe toward the goal which is common both to science and humanity — the welfare of man.

CONVOCATION ADDRESS

(Twentieth Convocation of the University of Waterloo May 29, 1970)

J. C. Polanyi

Dr. Polanyi is Professor of Chemistry at the University of Toronto.

Today's critical view of science is a more mature one than the view it replaced. Science, and more particularly the technology that it spawns, is, quite obviously, *not* automatically beneficent.

Science uncovers the laws of nature. Technology then devises the means to put these laws at our service, making us, in the short run, healthier, more powerful, mobile, and so forth. However, it remains true that we only discover the laws of nature; we cannot alter them. From these simple facts stem important consequences.

Francis Bacon, one of the great champions of technological progress through scientific research, remarked almost four centuries ago that, "Nature, to be commanded, must be obeyed." What he meant was that before we attempted to apply nature's laws we had better understand them. He gave an example from his own times. There is, he said, no use in trying to develop a process for converting mercury into gold, if you have not first taken the trouble to study the nature of mercury and the nature of gold. He was, as you can see, an early pro-

ponent of basic research as the bedrock on which scientific applications must rest. That particular lesson we have learnt over the intervening centuries (though our legislators are still prone to memory lapses on this fundamental point).

But there is more to it than that. What we now realize — and should have realized earlier — is that Francis Bacon's dictum is of much wider scope. "Nature, to be commanded, must be obeyed," he said. The mention of mercury, which was Bacon's example, strikes a familiar and distressing chord. Nature, in the form of mercury, has in recent years been commanded to perform various ingenious services for man, in the industries adjacent to Lake St. Clair and Lake Erie. However, the investigation of nature's laws as they applied to mercury once it left the immediate service of man, and seeped into the adjoining lakes, was inadequate. Nature's laws, it should have have been apparent, would continue to operate outside the walls of the factory. They operated, as it turned out, in such a fashion as to do a disservice to man. The mercury content of the lake-fish rose, as you know, to a distressingly high level. Nature (putting

Reprinted by permission of the author, John Polanyi.

it into Bacon's terms) was commanded at one point, without being obeyed at others.

Taken in the context of the full range of problems raised by modern technology — which include, among other horrors, the possibility of a world war involving nuclear, chemical, or biological weapons, and the likelihood of catastrophic famines due to over-population — the example I have chosen is trifling. I chose it because it is actual and recent.

The first question it raises in our minds is "who is to blame?" One thinks of the scientists and engineers in these industries. One thinks of the managers. One thinks of the government inspectors. It is impossible to exonerate any of them.

They are all guilty parties. But not quite in the way that it might appear. They are guilty, in the first place, not professionally, but as citizens. Their shortsightedness has been a faithful reflection of that of each one of us. So long as there was no effective public interest in the wider consequences of technological developments, there could not be any serious study of such questions.

The company that set its scientists and engineers to work on developing and testing a model of the ecological effects of various levels of mercury-containing effluents, would have no choice but to pass the costs of this undertaking on to its customers. Since the product would be no better, merely more expensive, the company would shortly go bankrupt, and would cease to exist. That would solve its pollution problem; greatly to the satisfaction of competing producers who had failed to take similar precautions.

In case you feel inclined to lay the blame for this outcome on the dog-eats-dog pattern of our competitive economy, let me say that the Soviet Union is also severely troubled by problems of industrial pollution. Recently Izvestia was deploring the existence of many thousands "of dairy factories, fish factories, tanneries, linen factories, regional food-combines and industrial complexes . . . nearly all of [which] have no waste water purifying installations." You may not be much disturbed by the steep increase in the cost of Russian caviar. It is relevent, nonetheless, since it is traceable to the fact that huge amounts of oil and sewage are being dumped into the Caspian Sea. Whether you are a socialist sturgeon in the Caspian or a capitalist pickerel in Lake Erie, your chances of being poisoned, it would appear, are entirely comparable. The fault lies in what has been, until very recently, a world-wide phenomenon of ignorance and consequently of indifference to the secondary effects of technological progress.

What is to be done? It is too late to beat a retreat from the world of technology back into a state of nature. The cliché of "space-ship earth" is trite, but telling. What it expresses is that we have by now made the earth into an instrument of man. We have done this in our attempt to better the human condition. The attempt has had enormous successes, but it has at the same time placed us in great peril. If something goes wrong in a space-ship in flight, one no longer has the option of simply retiring to the country. . . .

We can only combat technology with more technology. This may sound like a counsel of despair, but it is not. It is, in fact, already a part of life. When your car breaks down, you get it repaired; you do not, in general, buy a horse. The difference is that the sorts of technological breakdown which we now anticipate are of a type which must be repaired to a large extent in advance, or they will be irreparable.

To help us do this we must abandon the pursuit of some of our most mindless technology, in favor of mindful technology. One thinks at once of the world expenditure on new weapons, which continues year by year to increase at a rate higher than (even) the population growth, and faster than the growth in world productivity. In the four years from 1963 to '67 the world expenditure on armaments increased by almost one-third. It now amounts to about $300 per year for every family on earth, or very roughly three times the average family income in India.

This is certainly not the only source of funds for environmental research, but it is an obvious one. Let me give one example. It would be unfair to call it an example of mindless research, but it is an example of a case where shifting attitudes can and should be turned to mankind's advantage.

In the past year the United States spent several hundred million dollars on research, development, testing, and procurement of chemical and biological weapons. We in Canada supported a program of research in chemical and biological warfare at the Defence Research Establishment in Suffield, Alberta. The Suffield establishment has some millions of dollars worth of plant, 1,000 square miles of land, and a budget last year of over $4 million.

A senior scientist at the Suffield labs, remarked with feeling recently that ". . . we're in a business that we all wish we didn't have to have." Things have been happening to suggest that we do not have to have this business.

Six months ago President Nixon renounced, on behalf of the United States, the use of biological weapons under any circumstances whatever, and began the implementation of a program for the destruction of existing stocks. He announced that he would send to the U.S. Senate for ratification the 1925 Geneva Protocol prohibiting the first use of chemical weapons. More recently, on March 24 of this year, Mr. George Ignatieff, Canada's delegate to the 25 nation Geneva disarmament conference, went further than this; he read a statement on behalf of the Canadian Government in which an undertaking was made not to "develop, produce, acquire, stockpile or use" either biological *or chemical* weapons, unless these weapons were used first against Canada or its allies.

Examined closely this statement is rather mysterious. Is it our intention to start the "development, production . . ." etc. of chemical weapons at the first whiff of enemy gas? I am not deeply concerned about this apparent illogicality. In diplomacy good sense should take precedence over logic. The motive behind the Canadian declaration, as I understand it, makes eminently good sense. It aims to strengthen the psychological barrier against the use of chemical weapons — a barrier which is presently being eroded, sad to say, by the extensive military use of tear gas and herbicides in Vietnam (some 10 million pounds of tear gas and roughly 100 million pounds of defoliant, up till now, in an area about equal to that of Vancouver Island).

This psychological barrier is vitally important to the future development of world armaments. The weapons of chemical warfare are relatively cheap and accessible. If ever the reluctance to use them is overcome, the danger of their proliferation around the world will be great; very much greater than that of nuclear weapons.

22

The requirements of diplomacy are at one with logic in demanding that Mr. Igantieff's sweeping renunciation of chemical and biological warfare should be seen to have a real impact on Canada's research in the area of CBW.

The objective of the Suffield CBW research establishment has, it is true, been described as "defensive." The claim is a fair one in a world where even hydrogen bombs can be arguably described as defensive. Nonetheless we have reached a juncture where the facilities of such laboratories could better be used as one of the instruments required to defend us against the chemical warfare that we are beginning to wage against ourselves. One thinks, for example, of the pressing need for the development and testing of substitutes for potentially dangerous pesticides such as DDT.

Pesticides fall within the competence of the Suffield establishment. Several of the most important chemical weapons were in fact discovered about 30 years ago in the course of chemical research into insecticides. The technological traffic can just as well move in the reverse direction. The choice is ours. In fact the Suffield establishment, as part of its CBW program, succeeded some years ago in developing effective vaccines against animal plagues, which have proved to be of great value in Asia and India. This suggests the possibility that a newly oriented Suffield research center might either be placed under the Ministry of Health and Welfare or be made part of the very ambitious research program now being inaugurated by the Canadian International Development Agency.

I have dwelt at some length on a single proposal. It is not even a very major one. My intention has been to illustrate that we do have saner options open to us, if we look for them, and press for them, with courage and imagination.*

Nothing could be more damaging than the despairing view, which claims that modern technology cannot help but lead to disaster. In one day's newspaper (to give an example) the computer is credited with the power to reduce us all to the level of anonymous statistics. In the next day's paper we are warned of the opposite danger; that the computer will lay bare every detail of our private lives. Of course both these outcomes, as well as many happier ones, are possible. It is up to us to determine what the outcome shall be.

Let me give a final example, to illustrate what I fear in today's mood. If Gregor Mendel were to announce the discovery of the laws of heredity in 1970 from the biology department of MIT, instead of 100 years ago from the kitchen garden of an Augustinian monastery, the newspapers would be black with headlines warning of the imminent danger of government manipulation of population, through state-controlled breeding. Again they would be right, in that the possibility exists; the Nazis tried it, and the South Africans are doing so today. But in neither case did technology compel them to take this course; the choice was clearly that of men. Men in some parts of the world acting foolishly, ignorantly, or with evil intent, but in most of the world (in this instance) acting with restraint and humanity.

The cure for misapplied technology is not to be found in a panic-stricken flight from technology, but in well-applied technology. The responsibility rests with us all.

*(Mr. Nixon's recent proposal that the vast riches of the seabed, at depths greater than 200 metres, be put into international trusteeship for the benefit of all mankind, if implemented, would be a magnificent example of a step in the right direction).

Part 2

By "progress," we frequently mean the acquisition by man of a variety of labour-saving devices — washing machines, automobiles, airplanes, etc. One used to hear people speak of man "taming nature" — using the forces of nature for man's own purposes. Of late, this phrase has fallen into disrepute as we have become aware that nature has not been tamed, but raped. Man's purposes are obviously not the same as nature's. We have become aware that our "gadgets" have helped to save us from some back-breaking labour, but have also provided unwanted by-products in the form of wastes pumped into the air or the water without regard for the consequences. It is only in the last decade or so that voices have been raised warning of the dangers facing us.

WARNING!
THIS WATER IS POLLUTED
NOT SAFE
FOR
BATHING

St. Catharines-Lincoln Health Unit

MANKIND'S FOULED NEST

Edward Cowan

Mr. Cowan, a foreign correspondent for The New York Times, now based in Toronto, covered the wreck of the Torrey Canyon for that paper and wrote of it in greater detail in Oil and Water: The Torrey Canyon Disaster (*Lippincott*).

Oil on the Waters

The escape of oil from Union Oil's offshore well opposite Santa Barbara, Calif., and the subsequent chain of events, political and natural, should be read as an object lesson in humility. The leak, the difficulties in plugging it, and the quick dashing of hopes that the shore line would be spared serious pollution, are all reminders that man has repeatedly and injuriously lost control of his own inventions, usually when he least expected to.

Fred J. Hartley, the aggresive marketing man who is president of Union Oil Company of California (record 1968 profits of $151.2 million on $1.9 billion of sales), argued that the eruption that produced the leak could not reasonably have been anticipated. Perhaps not. Nor could the loss of a hydrogen bomb over Spain. Nor the 1965 Northeast power failure. Nor the stranding two years ago of the supertanker *Torrey Canyon,* whose captain ran her onto a well-marked granite reef off England in broad daylight, causing the biggest shipwreck and oil pollution ever. Nor, just a year after that, the

stranding and breakup of another Liberian flag tanker, the *Ocean Eagle,* at the entrance to San Juan harbour — hardly an uncharted shoal.

Surely no one could reasonably have expected in November, 1968, that an oil barge carrying more than 1 million gallons of heavy fuel oil would be torn loose from its tow by rough weather and grounded on Rehoboth Beach, Del., where Washingtonians soak up the summer sun. Or that, also last November, a Standard Oil of California hose would rupture and let 60,000 gallons of diesel oil pour into Humboldt Bay, not far from Eureka, Calif.

Who could reasonably be called on to anticipate that a 365-foot tanker would break in two in the Panama Canal in December, 1968, losing some of its cargo of fuel oil? Or that two days before Christmas, the little tanker *Mary A. Whalen* would run aground off Rockaway Point, N.Y., on the south shore of Long Island, hard by New York City's most heavily used stretch of beaches? Or that on Christmas Day Japanese authorities would have to close the Naruto Strait because of the danger to ships from gasoline that had escaped from a grounded tanker?

Who might reasonably be expected to warn the Coast Guard that quantities of what appeared to be heavy fuel oil would wash up onto the Rhode Island coast on Inauguration Day, 1969 —

Reprinted with permission of *The Nation,* March 10, 1969 by Edward Cowan.

25

but that there would be no clue to the ship or shore plant from which it escaped?

As any lawyer can quickly point out, there are differences in the origins of these several disasters which are worth defining if one is concerned about writing useful public policy. There are acts of God, such as violent storms; there is human error, such as putting a tanker on a known reef; there is the inevitable breakdown in any man-made mechanical system, such as the tendency of tankers with riveted sides (a construction technique largely discontinued about six years ago, according to one expert) to ooze oil around the rivets. That leakage may be only a barrel a day, but a barrel of crude oil, thick and persistent stuff, may be more than a drop in the ocean. In the Rehoboth Beach incident, the barge that was washed ashore lost, from a pipe that broke, a quantity of oil described by Interior Department officials as "very small" somewhere from 5 to 30 barrels. That "very small" dose of heavy oil, according to the officials, "marked" 2 to 3 miles of beach and caused substantial pollution to about three blocks of beach front.

Looking back over the two years since the *Torrey Canyon* disaster alerted the public and governments to the dangers inherent in the transportation of vast quantities of crude oil, it is startling to observe how many pollution incidents and near misses there have been; the list just recited is far from exhaustive.

It was instructive, for example, to learn from a trade publication this winter of two tanker casualties off southern Africa in the spring of 1968. On April 29, about 3 miles off the Cape of Good Hope, the *Esso Essen* struck an underwater obstruction and cut herself open at three points. She lost about 30,000 barrels of Arabian heavy crude

oil. Esso said it applied its new dispersant, Corexit, "with great success." In the other reported casualty, the tanker *Andron*, whose owner is listed as a Greek company, split a seam in heavy seas. After discharging her cargo of Kuwait crude, she underwent temporary repairs at Durban, reloaded the oil, resumed her voyage for Venice, and sank about 10 miles off Southwest Africa. Exactly what happened to her cargo of about 16,000 tons (117,000 barrels) is not fully known but there are only two possibilities; immediate or gradual pollution of the sea.

In short, with the world's consumption of petroleum products — in homes, factories, office buildings, schools, chemical plants, aircraft, ships, motor vehicles and electric generating stations — increasing by 7.5 percent a year (it is now seven times what it was in 1938), the waterborne shipment of oil has become an industry in itself. Twenty-five years ago, the *T-2*, workhorse tanker of World War II, carried about 16,000 tons. By the early 1960s, Japanese shipyards, emerging as the world's busiest, were building ships to cary more than 100,000 tons and were "stretching" smaller ships. The *Torrey Canyon*, for example, built at Newport News, Va., to carry 67,000 tons was jumboized in Japan to carry 118,000 tons. By keeping her original power plant and propulsion system, the most expensive part of a tanker, the *Torrey Canyon*, at only a slight sacrifice of speed, nearly doubled her delivery capacity. The saving worked out to roughly a penny a barrel. Show any international oil company how to add a penny a barrel to profits and it can make you very rich by cutting you in for only a few daubs of the extra icing.

The same economic logic lifted tanker size to 312,000 tons by 1968 with the launching of the *Universe Ire-*

land, first of six such ships to be operated by Gulf. Last November the Japanese yard that built her, Ishikawa-jima-Harima Heavy Industries Co., got an order for a 370,000-tonner, to cost between $22 million and $25 million. Disputing some industry experts, the buyer, Tokyo Tanker Co., said it thought that economies of scale would persist as capacity approached 500,-000 tons.

The 370,000-ton tanker will carry three times as much oil as did the *Torrey Canyon*. The 50,000 tons or more of oil that she spilled contaminated 140 miles of English coast and a considerable stretch of Brittany's northern shore, 110 miles from the wreck.

Could a *Torrey Canyon* disaster occur again? Like today's new supertankers, she was well made and equipped with modern navigational aids. She stranded solely as the result of her captain's bad seamanship — "an aberration," one expert mariner called the performance. If it seemed too incredible to happen more than once in a lifetime, one had only to wait a year for the captain of the *Ocean Eagle*, which split in two, to fracture her bottom on the ocean floor in front of San Juan harbor.

Britain's aerial bombing of the *Torrey Canyon* (an attempt successful, said Whitehall, to burn the oil remaining in her tanks) and the struggle by troops and civilians to remove inches of oil from beaches and harbors attracted hundreds of newsmen. Overnight, governments, editors and the public discovered how much oil a single ship can carry; how persistent, noxious and, for waterfowl, lethal, crude oil can be; how emotional can be the argument about how to clean it up, with tourism-minded merchants advocating chemicals for a quick, thorough wash, and fishermen and nat-uralists preferring mechanical methods; how unprepared, in law and in practical arrangements, national states are to cope with, much less put an end to, oil pollution.

In the United States, the *Torrey Canyon* episode and unrelated instances of pollution to the New Jersey and Cape Cod shores a few weeks later dramatized not only the enormity of the (infrequent) major disaster but the fact that coastal oil pollution is an everyday problem. Despite efforts of the big tanker fleets to dispose of their residues innocuously, there is a lot of clandestine bilge washing by countless freighters, trawlers and tankers.

These events fired up a mood of reform in Washington. President Johnson directed the Secretaries of Transportation and Interior to make a study of oil pollution and recommend legislation. A number of Congressmen — and lobbyists — began to gird themselves for another round in the continuing conflict between public and private interest. In London, meanwhile, an emergency session of the Inter-Governmental Maritime Consultative Organization (IMCO), a UN body, had been convened at Britain's request. It began deliberations on two conventions to supplement existing international law. One would establish the right of a state to take action against a foreign-owned ship lying offshore, but in international waters, to protect the state's coast from pollution. (Britain, despite the readiness of the Royal Navy to try to fire the leaking *Torrey Canyon* immediately, stood aside for ten days of fruitless salvage attempts, in part because there was no legal authority or precedent for destroying someone else's property on the high seas.) The other convention would establish liability of ship owners for pollution damage. With uncommon dispatch, IMCO also adopted a package of recommendations to national states on technical safety matters and on tougher enforcement of anti-pollution law.

Another aspect of the tanker business that was illuminated by the *Torrey Canyon* and *Ocean Eagle* casualties is the role of the Republic of Liberia as the world's leading country in registered merchant marine tonnage. In 1947, because of difficulties with Panamanian consuls who, owners said, sought to collect "fees" every time a Panamanian-flag ship cleared their ports, United States shipping interests were looking for a new flag of convenience (or flag of necessity, depending on how one chooses to approach the wage and tax argument). That need coincided with the engagement of the late Edward R. Stettinius, Jr., to assist Liberia's economic development. The result was the drafting by three Wall Street law firms of legislation, duly enacted in Monrovia, that put Liberia in the business of registering ships.

In the ensuing twenty years, Liberia has taken great pains to rebut trade union accusations that hers is a "runaway flag", flown by unsafe, leaky old tubs whose crews are virtually galley slaves and incompetent, too. Without getting into that argument, it can be said that the jumbo tankers which today fly the Liberian flag are well-made vessels. The African state has what seem to be exacting regulations governing seaworthiness, loading and safety equipment. It issues officers' papers either reciprocally or after an applicant passes examinations which Liberia says are tougher than those of other countries. Liberia, says Albert J. Rudick, an American lawyer who is employed full time in New York with a staff of forty as Liberian Deputy Commissioner of Maritime Affairs, tries to make a ship owner's responsibilities commensurate with the benefits (no corporate income tax) of the Liberian flag.

Nevertheless, the Liberian maritime program remains very much as it was conceived — an affair for the benefit of American ship owners and quietly managed by them and their lawyers who decide, without "benefit" of public scrutiny or debate, how to balance private and public interest. (Mr. Rudick argued that there is meaningful debate in Liberia's Congress but he was unable to name the relevant committees or their chairmen.)

When the *Torrey Canyon's* board of investigation met, it had no rules of procedure to follow. Its mandate was a regulation for inquiries which stresses the possible negligence of the crew and thereby underplays the possible role in a casualty of the ship's mechanical condition or of acts or omissions by its owners. No wonder that the board failed to mention in its report certain things it learned about the condition and equipping of the ship — matters now very relevant to damage suits by Britain and France against the *Torrey Canyon's* owner (a phantom Liberian corporation with head office in Bermuda) and operator, Union Oil, Nor, one supposes, is it surprising that nearly a year after the *Ocean Eagle* casualty the report of investigation had not been released by Monrovia, where, it was explained, they have been very busy this winter celebrating William V.S. Tubman's twenty-fifth anniversary as President.

Similarly, Liberia has not released for discussion changes in its laws and regulations, soon to be put into effect. Surely, the maritime rules of the foremost "seafaring nation" are of interest outside Monrovia; but, except in Wall Street where the proposed changes were drafted, they are generally unknown.

The overriding issue posed by the *Torrey Canyon* disaster, the *Ocean Eagle* episode, the eruption of the well opposite Santa Barbara, and lesser instances of pollution is that of responsibility. Shall a tanker, drilling rig, shore installation (e.g., refinery, transshipment terminal, depot, etc.) or other oil facility be responsible for damage done by its oil? Shall it be responsible absolutely, that is, regardless of whether or not it is at fault, or only if negligent? And if liable shall it pay the full damages, or only up to a limited amount?

The questions are being debated in London at IMCO meetings of legal experts and in Washington in hearings before the subcommittee on air and water pollution of the Senate Public Works Committee. One of the conventions that IMCO experts hope will be completed at Brussels next November would deal with the liability of tankers for oil damage. The Brussels conference will have to decide how sweeping the liability shall be. A slight majority of the deliberating nations, including the United States, is said to favor absolute liability. More likely, the process of accommodation will produce liability based on fault, with the burden of proof on the ship.

The amount of liability will be limited, partly because it traditionally has been and partly because of the expense and difficulties of getting insurance for unlimited liability. How high the limitation should be will also be resolved at the conference. The United States has proposed two to four times the 1957 liability convention limit of $67 a gross registered ton, with a maximum of $15 million (Washington has never signed that convention.) The International Maritime Committee, a small, little-known, powerful Antwerp-based network of lawyers, which has drafted several important maritime conventions, is expected to press for its 1957 formula or not much more. Undoubtedly, all opening positions on this point were taken for bargaining

purposes. The issue may be argued as one of how damge can be reasonably expected, with cleanup costs from various spills offered in evidence. At bottom, it is a matter of tanker owners and operators trying to minimize their extra insurance costs. Washington estimates the convention may add 10 percent to a tanker's normal insurance costs, or about 2 percent to operating costs. A 2 percent rise in operating costs in any business is not trivial.

The same question has arisen before the Senate subcommittee, which is considering legislation (S.7) sponsored by its chairman, Senator Muskie. It would, among other things, authorize the government to clean up oil spills in inland and territorial waters and require the tanker to pay the costs. The legislation proposes a limit of $450 a ton up to $15 million. Asserting that these levels would "amount to a denial of ship owners' right to limitation of liability," the Maritime Law Association of the United States, representing some 2,000 admiralty lawyers (who generally work for ship owners) urged the Congress to return to the $67 a ton and $5 million limits written in legislation passed by the Senate and weakened by the House Public Works Committee (where an oil man and a shipping man held sway) in 1968. The American Petroleum Institute proposed $100 a ton up to $10 million. Last year it proposed $250 a ton up to $8 million. It changed its mind, it said, to go along with the limits adopted by seven major oil companies which have established a voluntary cleanup plan (which will come into effect only if a lot more tanker owners adhere). An API tabulation showed that the most expensive cleanup on record — for the tanker *General Colocotronis* in the Bahamas a year ago — was $800,000. Conveniently, the API explicitly excluded the *Torrey Canyon*, whose cleanup expense it put at $8 million (half the claims of Britain and France), because of "technological progress over the past two years and many of the mistakes made in the *Torrey Canyon* incident would not be repeated, and, of course, research on cleanup methods is continuing." Those few words hardly justify ignoring $7.2 million of an $8 million cleanup bill.

The Maritime Law Association, seeking to establish limitation as something close to divine right, argued that it "is rooted in the universally recognized principle that it is of paramount consideration for maritime nations to preserve the continuity of maritime commerce as a matter of vital national interest." The association, noting that Congress granted limitation in 1851 (the legislation has not been significantly altered since then), went on to cite an 1871 Supreme Court decision which recognized that the law's object was "to induce capitalists to invest" in ships.

The argument could hardly be less relevant. Even if the asserted "paramount consideration" exists, it does not necessarily follow that it applies to the United States or that commerce cannot be sustained in foreign-flag bottoms, which are sent to sea to make a buck and presumably will be available. As for any national security argu-ment. there is good reason (if only the multiplicity of pressures Washington can bring to bear) to believe that American-owned ships under foreign flags would be available in time of urgent need. As for persuading that legendary capitalist to invest in ships, the argument antedates common use of the corporation, when the investor was personally liable for the ship's damage, and the development of today's broad, deep, versatile insurance market. Because of these changed economic conditions, limitation is not so just, necessary or immutable as its beneficiaries argue. According to some qualified lawyers, the courts are moving away from it.

The Santa Barbara mishap and Senator Muskie's bill are forcing the Nixon Administration to review offshore drilling policy and regulation, and also what is known about materials and techniques for cleaning up spilled oil on sea and land without harming natural life. With the oil industry itself accepting Senator Muskie's principle that the government should be reimbursed for cleaning up spills arising from private commerce, it would seem likely that the President will sign the bill — if it is not stranded on one of those hidden shoals in the House Public Works Committee.

OUR NEXT CHALLENGE:
TO MOVE A MOUNTAIN

In 1967, in a special issue of *The Globe Magazine* devoted to how that filthiest of animals, man, is ever going to clean up after himself, staff writer Betty Lee despairingly concluded that the only way might be to blast earth's garbage to the moon. About the only thing that has happened in the matter of refuse disposal since is that lunar flight has become a going concern. Hence, the big garbage dump in the sky?

Hardly. But something pretty drastic *has* to be done. Air pollution. Water pollution. Noise pollution. Add garbage. It is a tremendous problem in its own right and deserves to be as tremendous a cause. How to dispose of it has placed Metro Toronto in a "panic situation", Works Commissioner Ross Clark told Etobicoke Council the other day. He wanted to get it to approve building of a $10-million incinerator, complete with 400-foot stack, which would dispose of 1,000 tons of garbage a day. That's one quarter of the refuse produced in Metro.

Burning it is of course one way to get rid of the stuff — by converting it into air pollution spread over a nice large area by that stack. But it can only be a start. For instance, you can't burn the eight million cars that are junked annually in North America. Or the millions upon millions of bottles and cans and what have you that help make up the 17 million tons of garbage produced annually in Canada.

Consider this prospect:

If we somehow managed to remove all pollutants from the air, the resulting mass would weigh about 133 million tons. Where to put it?

In Metro, as generally in urban areas in the industrialized world, a little more than half the refuse is combustible and destroyed in incinerators. The biggest single item: paper and paper products. The rest just has to be dumped somewhere.

Just as people on the lakeshore are unhappy about having that huge incinerator, few want to live next to garbage dumps even under the euphemism sanitary landfill. Metro, for that matter, is fast running out of landfill sites. A new one is being made available at Pickering, it's true, but that is a long and costly haul.

Metro's proposed capital budget for 1970 provides $6,735,000 for garbage removal. It cannot be termed a waste of money, but the truth is that what we are getting for it can in no way be judged satisfactory — simply because man has not yet come up with a satisfactory way of cleaning up his mess. There have been stabs at it, that's all.

The Swedes, extraordinarily strong on environmental cleanliness, have made a couple of pretty spectacular ones. A few years ago, over the objections of fishing interests who feared ichthyological damage, they began to dispose of old cars simply by sailing

Reprinted from *The Globe and Mail*, Toronto, March 9, 1970.

31

them into the Baltic and dumping them overboard. They are also — and the British have picked up the idea — experimenting with transporting garbage by suction through underground pipelines to incerators. This takes care of the haulage problem, but there again is that end result: air pollution.

Instead of the Baltic, take Lake Ontario and turn it to more constructive use. Should we extend Metro's waterfront by adding much of the annual 1.5 million tons of garbage to other landfill material? A way may be found to keep putrefying refuse from contaminating the water, perhaps by compressing the stuff into dense blocks (the Japanese are experimenting with this process). One problem with garbage landfill so far is that it takes about 10 years to settle so that buildings can be erected on it.

As for incinerators, if burning there must be, Alderman Anthony O'Dono-

hue — an engineer who had studied garbage disposal in Europe — suggested in 1968 that they might be used to produce steam heat. This is being done successfully in Montreal, but Metro Council ignored the idea. It should be reviewed, for its merits would seem obvious: the heat could be sold, and producing it would cause less air pollution than the individual heating units it would replace.

A World Health Organization report has called garbage disposal mankind's ultimate problem. That may be somewhat hyperbolic in the age of the Bomb. Still, output of refuse has doubled since the Nineteen Twenties, and it is increasing in Metro Toronto and other industrial areas by 10 percent a year. Yet the only advance since Roman days in disposing of it has been the introduction of garbage grinders.

If you don't count flying to the moon.

BE TENDER WITH OUR TUNDRA

Lawrence C. Bliss

Mr. Bliss is a writer on scientific subjects and a frequent contributer to the Globe Magazine.

The Arctic tundra of North America has been little known to most of us until recently, largely because of its distance — a hostile and seemingly worthless environment as measured by our economically oriented society. This has all changed with the discovery of oil at Prudhoe Bay, Alaska. The immediate concern of most people inter-

ested in the North was how much oil is there, how can it be extracted and brought to the gasoline devouring market in southern Canada, the United States and Europe, and how much will it add to our gross national product.

Within months a winter road had been developed over the frozen tundra and plans were laid for the supertanker Manhattan to attempt to navigate the Arctic. Practically all of these decisions were based upon the economical feasi-

Reprinted by permission from *The Globe Magazine,* January 17, 1970.

bility of extracting and shipping the oil, the mechanical-technological feasibility of an Arctic tanker, Arctic drilling equipment and an Arctic pipeline, and the environmental feasibility of the total project — mentioned mostly by environmental scientists, though some companies are aware of their environmental problems and are seeking ecological help.

Most of the world's large oil fields developed to now have been in temperate or desert regions where relatively few problems of drilling, road construction and pipeline laying were encountered. When pipelines were buried, plants soon invaded the bare soil and healed the scars of man's manipulation. The Arctic is a far different environment combining very low winter temperatures, little winter daylight, frozen and snow covered ground and ice for 8 to 11 months per year, hordes of insects in the short summer, and permanently frozen soil to a depth of 600 to 2,000 feet. In summer the upper few inches or few feet thaw forming a soupy mass for heavy track or wheeled vehicles to traverse.

Many of the ecological problems in the Arctic stem from the harsh environment which greatly reduces the number of species that can live there and slows the growth rates of plants and animals. This means that the balance of nature is more easily upset, and once this occurs, it takes far longer for a new balance to be achieved. This is especially true of the growth of plants and the need to reduce disturbance of the surface.

In mid-latitudes we drive bulldozers and use chain saws with reckless abandon, for we know that plants will soon seal most road cuts and bulldozed strips, and that trees will grow again. In spite of this our fields are often badly eroded and our streams and rivers are full of silt. Most dams are built for a life expectancy of 30 to 50 years, not because the steel and concrete will last no longer, but because they fill with silt.

In the Arctic, if the plant cover is removed, more solar energy enters the darker colored surface and melts more of the permafrost. The vegetation acts as an insulative layer, especially the mosses called sphagnum. During the oil explorations and movement of people into the Arctic in the Nineteen Forties and early Fifties, bulldozers were used without this knowledge and severe thermal erosion, often with accelerated soil erosion, resulted in topography erosion called thermokarst. This condition comes about when vegetation growth is slower than the melting rate of the frozen ground.

Thus most material was moved by large cat trains only in winter, and little damage was done to the tundra. However, with the discovery of oil there was pressure to move more material faster and throughout the year. Much was taken north by plane and barge, but winter roads were used late into the spring; now large scars traverse the tundra of Alaska, and grow larger each year as more ground thaws and turns to a soupy mass.

Roads into the tundra must be built of gravel, but, as in temperate regions, engineers all too often clear away all the vegetation rather than lay the gravel on top so that after the vegetation dies it will continue to serve as an insulative layer.

As if these problems were not enough, there are the problems of oil transport by land or sea. The Manhattan voyage gave the public the impression of great success, that the Northwest Passage had at long last been conquered. The public relations personnel were most efficient, but the voyage was not what they made it out to be. The facts are that the Manhattan would not have reached Alaska without the accompanying ice breakers; it could not make the McClure Strait and its ice ridges, so it retreated to the less ice congested Prince of Wales Strait.

Furthermore, the ship made this voyage at the most favorable time of year and during the best (most ice-free) summer in more than 50 years. In spite of all of these favorable factors two large holes were put in its hull, which hardly indicate there's a good year-round oil transportation link between the Arctic and east coast and European markets. It's significant that the Manhattan returned south via the west coast and not back through the ice pack.

Even if huge tankers can traverse the ice pack at any season, there are the problems of building an Arctic port and getting the oil by pipeline to it, an offshore distance of 10 to 30 miles. In the nearshore region the line would have to be buried because of the onshore push of ice which could rupture even large pipes. Furthermore, the engineering design is far from complete.

Ecologically, the most serious problem is the danger of a ship sinking or breaking open at sea. The Torrey Canyon and Santa Barbara oil disasters were bad enough, but a tanker spilling thousands of tons of oil in the Arctic would be still worse. In temperate regions oil will decompose in time, but in the Arctic it could last for 30 to 50 years.

In the meantime, it would be disastrous to birds, seals, walrus, seashore insects and other invertebrates, and it could reduce photosynthetic rates (food production) of algae by reducing light penetration. All other organisms in the sea are directly or indirectly dependent upon algae for food. Thus the productivity of the Arctic sea could be seriously reduced.

The alternative to tankers is a pipeline. The line and route receiving most attention is the Trans Alaska Pipeline System (TAPS), which would take oil from Prudhoe Bay to Valdez on the south coast of Alaska via a 48-inch line. The engineering feasibility of this line has not been worked out with regard to potential earthquake damage in the Valdez area, a region of frequent earthquakes; neither have pipeline welding and positioning in relation to the Arctic and sub-Arctic permafrost.

Engineers predict that the oil will have a temperature of 150 to 160 degrees in the line and that friction along the line will keep it from cooling. They further predict that with heat loss the pipeline buried 3 feet below the surface will release enough heat to maintain surface soil temperatures of 70 degrees in winter and 130 degrees in summer. Under such temperature conditions, no plants will grow. Much of the line is projected to run along the river valleys where some of the problems are less difficult, but it will have to traverse areas of peaty, high ice content permafrost where the pipe must be insulated. Nevertheless their plans do not call for insulation.

If the line were placed on top of the ground it would act as a huge fence blocking the movement of animals. If it were elevated, there is no assurance they would pass beneath. The line will have to pass through the Brooks Range and the Alaska Range, both of which will be difficult to cope with from an engineering point of view, and are potentially in danger of great ecological damage to the landscape because of much rock blasting. Even south of the Alaska Range there is much permafrost within the forested areas which will create further problems of heat loss, permafrost melt and thermokarst development.

The pipeline will need a service road for construction, inspection, and emergency repairs. The road would appear to be best located next to the line, but this would place it in the valleys where it will be flooded out and inaccessible each spring. If placed in the wet soil uplands it will disturb more tundra and not provide easy access to the valleys. If the line ruptures, much oil can be lost in river waters unless automatic shutoff valves are installed at frequent intervals.

Once the oil reaches Valdez it will be stored in huge tanks for shipment by tanker to Seattle or further south. The tanks, while well constructed, will not be earthquake proof and vast damage to wildlife would be caused should they rupture during the 20 to 30 year period the fields are expected to pump oil. The probability of pollution from earthquakes is very high.

As an alternative the Mackenzie Valley pipeline would run east from Prudhoe Bay to Inuvik south to Edmonton where existing lines could initially carry the crude to the midwest. This line would have to cross the Alaska Wildlife Refuge or south of the Brooks and east to the Mackenzie.

Assuming that oil is found in the delta, a trunk line would then join the main line.

This line, though not as far along in its development, has been engineered with a greater understanding and concern for the ecology of the North. Its further advantage is that it would deliver oil directly to the market and not run into the dangerous pollution problems of shipping and the construction of a new line across the United States. In the December 1, 1969, issue of *Oilweek* the estimated costs per barrel from Prudhoe Bay to Chicago are $1.05 via Alaska and tanker to Seattle versus 55 cents via the Mackenzie line. The cost via Arctic supertankers is estimated to run $1.10 to the east coast ports. The Mackenzie pipeline is by far the cheapest, and ecologically it has the

potential of doing the least damage to the Arctic and sub-Arctic landscapes.

There are, however, a great many unsolved problems, so no release for a pipeline or tanker route should be given until both the Canadian and U.S. governments have spelled out land management and environmental control policies and weighed alternative routes and methods for oil removal. The companies must spell out in detail what their engineering plans are and alternative engineering designs must be considered in advance of decision making. The Resolutions of the Edmonton conference (October 15-17) on Productivity and Conservation in Northern Circumpolar Lands, pointed out that economic and social developments are often implemented at a speed which outpaces our ability to obtain necessary information on which to base rational land and resource management decisions.

The problem that society faces is that the oil industry spends vast sums of money on exploration, land leasing, drilling, and oil transport. This all results in great pressure to develop fields as fast as they are discovered so that company earnings do not suffer and pressure for maintaining inefficient combustion engines which further pollute our air.

We need counter-pressures to keep these valuable pools of hydrocarbons for future use in drug, textile, plastic and other industries rather than as an inefficient source of energy now. Decisions on the use of our resources must be based on criteria other than current economic and engineering feasibility. The total long term needs for these resources must be evaluated now. No nation can be great if it uses its resources with little thought for the future.

Ecological and environmental management decisions and feasibility must get as much attention as economic and engineering aspects — unless society is willing to continue paying high taxes and corporations lower dividends in an attempt to cure environment disorder after the damage has been done. The

Arctic can serve as a turning point in the way in which governments, industry and society approach the total problems of resource development. The question is will they.

WITHIN THE LAW

Lethal levels of chemical pollution have caused the death of 10,000 sea birds washed up in the Irish Sea over the past two months. The chemicals, derived from chlorine and known as PCBs, are used in plastics, paints and cosmetics and turn up in many industrial effluents. The normal concentration of PCBs in most animal life is around ten parts in a million but concentrations twenty times as high are being found in the dead birds. Sadly, it is not possible to point to any accidental or illegal dumping of the chemical that could explain the deaths like it explained the death of fish in the Rhine. It seems that the pollution has built up entirely within the framework of the law.

The royal commission to look into the pollution of the environment, which the Prime Minister announced on Thursday, will concern itself with how far the law should be changed, and like all royal commissions, is likely to take its time. The more immediate issue is whether the existing law is being enforced as well as it might. The

answer is almost certainly that it is not. Twelve different departments at present dabble in the subject; the most important of them, coming under the aegis of the Ministry of Housing and Local Government, being the river authorities. Almost all the 4,500 million gallons of water that are daily polluted by domestic or industrial use pour into rivers and tidal waters. And the law leaves it to each authority to decide what levels of pollution it will allow. There are 29 river authorities; they all act independently, are all subject to local pressures, and so far have been slow to use anything like the full powers given to them under the Clean Rivers Act of 1961. Some even complain that the equipment needed to measure the chemicals in their water is too expensive to buy. So the situation could be even worse than we suspect. This is where some action is going to be expected of Mr. Anthony Crosland's new ministry; he is already setting up two advisory panels, one for farm chemicals in the post-DDT era and another for noise.

Reprinted with permission from *The Economist*, December 13, 1969.

OUR POLLUTED BAY

Hugh Whittington

Hugh Whittington is a staff reporter for the Hamilton Spectator.

Industrial and domestic pollution enters the bay through 15 municipally owned sewers.

For the reason, look back several years, when sewers were built to carry both storm water and sanitary sewage for discharge directly into the bay.

In recent years, the city has begun to replace the combined sewers with separate sewers for each function. But in many older areas of the city, the combined sewers still exist.

In order to protect the sewage collection system and sewage plant, major trunk sewers and pumping facilities were equipped with overflow by-pass pipes. Thus, under conditions of heavy flow, these by-passes divert excessive amounts of untreated sewage to the bay.

In Hamilton, a large number of storm sewer outfall pipes which discharge to the bay are used as receivers for by-passed sewage. In particular the east-west Burlington Street sanitary sewer has many such connections along its length.

OWRC's researchers studied these storm-sanitary sewage outlets into the bay and this is what they found in the bay around the outlets:

- Queen Street — fecal wastes present.
- Hess and Caroline — oil on surface and bottom. Bad odors. Human excrement visible.
- Simcoe — industrial and fecal pollution.
- James — industrial and fecal pollution. Human excrement visible.
- Catharine — no visible wastes. Fecal pollution indicated.
- Ferguson — industrial and fecal pollution.
- Wellington — bad odors. Human excrement visible. Severe pollution from industrial and domestic sources. Build-up of fecal solids on bottom.
- Wentworth — no settling problem. Some industrial and domestic pollution evident.
- Hillyard — bad odors. Fecal wastes and oil present. Build-up of fecal solids on bottom. Industrial pollution.
- Birch — large amounts of oil. Industrial and fecal pollution. No long-term settling problem.
- Gage — extensive fecal and severe industrial pollution. No long-term settling.
- Ottawa — bad odor with suspended solids and extensive oil. Fecal pollution. Long-term settling of fecal solids.
- Kenilworth — human exrement

Reprinted with permission of *The Hamilton Spectator,* May 24, 1969 by Hugh Whittington.

visible. Foul odors. Gas bubbles. Severe fecal pollution with some industrial.

• Strathearne — heavy scum. Gas bubbles. Human excrement visible. Severe fecal and industrial pollution. Heavy algae growth. No long-term settling.

• Parkdale — human excrement visible. Heavy algae growth. Fecal and industrial pollution.

In eight of the storm sewer outfalls mentioned, OWRC researchers could determine an actual flow into the bay . . . at Queen, James, Catharine, Wellington, Birch, Kenilworth, Strathearne and Parkdale.

They found that an average of 10,095 pounds of solid organic material were flowing into the bay from these outlets each day.

They added the 17,689 pounds of solid organic matter flowing from the Woodward Avenue sewage treatment plant, to arrive at a total of 27,784 pounds — about 13⅓ tons. That does not include any pollutants discharged directly into the bay by industry.

The major contributor of pollution during the period of study was the Strathearne Street sewer. More than three tons of organic matter — equal to the daily organic contribution of 37,000 persons — is estimated to have been entering the bay from this source on the day of sampling.

This and other organic discharge figures would, in all probability, be proportionally larger during periods of more intensive rainfall.

"For purposes of comparison during 1967 the partially treated sewage being discharged from the primary type sewage treatment plant averaged the equivalent organic contributions of slightly over 100,000 persons daily," the report states. "Sewage contributions of 6,660 and 6,000 persons have been estimated as the equivalent discharges from the Wellington Street and Kenilworth Avenue storm sewers respectively.

"The presence of this pollution indicates that either the by-pass facilities are not properly constructed, the collector system is of inadequate size to contain normal flows, or that there are direct sanitary and industrial connections to the storm sewers."

The report says: "It is obvious from the analytical data that pollution from industrial sources is being discharged to Hamilton Bay in significant quantities through storm sewer outfalls.

"Such pollutants should not be present during periods of dry weather as was experienced during the survey.

"Shoreline pollution was indicated by high bacterial counts and various observations of fecal solids and industrial contaminants. A long-term buildup of sanitary wastes on the bottom of the bay was evident opposite the discharge points at Ferguson, Wellington, Hillyard and Ottawa Streets.

"Severe pollution from fecal wastes was apparent in the vicinity of Hess, Caroline, Wellington and Hillyard Streets, and Birch, Gage, Kenilworth and Strathearne Avenues.

"Extensive industrial pollution was apparent at Wellington and Ottawa Streets, and Birch and Gage Avenues."

The eight major storm sewers under study were also analyzed to determine what chemical elements were evident.

There were chromium, copper, lead, iron, detergent components and phenols in all, but cadmium and cyanide in some.

SMOKE —
BUT NO FIRE YET

The common market has just announced it wants to control pollution from motor vehicles. This will help many motor manufacturers. It is nonsense for them to have to retool every time a fresh country wakes up to pollution (often to keep out foreign manufacturers as much as to reduce fumes). Equally, however, it is worth pointing out that nobody has yet proved that fumes from motor cars actually are a health hazard in Europe. Here is an excellent example of how the facts are getting lost in an environmental debate.

California, where this story began, is in a unique position. Apart from its very dense motor car population, it has bright sunlight and still air, encouraged by geographical factors. The Los Angeles smog, which is harmful to health, is directly attributable to these causes, but the same conditions are seldom likely to occur elsewhere. Petrol fumes have four ingredients that could be harmful: unburned petrol and hydrocarbons (arising from the fact that petrol engines are an inefficient form of combustion), carbon monoxide, oxides of nitrogen, and lead. Research in Britain, notably at St. Bartholomew's Hospital, has failed to substantiate harm from any of these.

For example, under the British Factories Act the critical level of carbon monoxide is 50 parts per million for an eight-hour exposure. Six of Britain's busiest and highly congested streets were chosen for an air sampling experiment (with pipes sticking out from walls at a height where little boys couldn't put marbles down them). But only on one or two occasions was the critical amount of carbon monoxide exceeded, and then only for 10-15 minutes. Other tests have shown that policemen on point duty are no more likely to suffer from lung complaints than anyone else.

All the same, fumes are unpleasant, and the health hazard cannot be ruled out entirely at this stage of the research. Some of the motor manufacturers have now come round to the idea that fumes must be cut anyway — otherwise they will sell fewer cars. But how to do it, and how much will it cost? The manufacturers say an air pump could cost as little as £1, if mass-produced, for some models. This would cope with carbon monoxide. But some outside experts say it would increase the oxides of nitrogen. A proper system of control might, they say, cost £40 a car.

Reprinted with permission from *The Economist*, November 16, 1969.

SURVEY INDICATES AVERAGE COTTAGE WORST POLLUTER OF ONTARIO'S LAKES

Thomas Claridge

Thomas Claridge is a staff reporter for the Globe and Mail.

The worst polluter of recreational lakes tends to be the modern cottage with its inadequate sewage disposal system.

Surveys of 13 recreational lakes in different parts of the province have shown that in many cases the septic tank is barely large enough to handle toilets wastes and the cottager often elects to send all other waste waters into leaching pits or even directly into the lake.

Until now the only significant policing in most cottage areas by local health authorities has been in response to complaints.

In most instances the cottager's original intention was to have a minimum of conveniences — perhaps nothing more than hydro and a pit privy. And unless there was subdivision control over the land in question he was pretty well free to do as he pleased in the provision of sanitary facilities.

Years later, when he decided to convert the cottage into a home away from home, he tended to install the facilities first and worry about sewage disposal later.

The effect on the lakes of laundry wastes draining directly into them has never been calculated, although surveys this summer of Stony and Clear lakes in the Kawarthas may give some indication. However, in the event the cottager uses a high-phosphate detergent the nutrient loading will be considerable and the contribution to algae growth undeniable.

Dr. W. H. (Wilf) Bennett, medical officer of health for Muskoka — Parry Sound Health Unit, can give a long list of reasons why his health unit can't do more. In fact, a chart used by his public health inspectors lists 60 categories of inspections that must be made under law.

"Last year we made a total of 4,300 septic tank inspections as a result of complaints beside approving over 1,000 new units," he said in a recent interview at his office in Bracebridge.

The health unit last year had to withdraw an offer to make pre-construction inspections of all cottage sites. The reason was a shortage of qualified public health inspectors, a shortage

Reprinted from *The Globe and Mail*, Toronto, June 29, 1970.

that persists in all health units not based in large cities.

Dr. Bennett told municipal councils in a letter sent last May 22 that it would be impossible to resume pre-construction checks of sites until the unit had two qualified inspectors at each of five branch offices. "Although eight sanitation assistants have been approved for the summer, the workload required for our qualified inspectors is still excessive and results in a backlog."

In the absence of pre-site inspections it is up to the subdivider or individual cottagers to make sure they have an adequate sewage disposal system. The health unit continues to check the systems on completion and can order changes.

Farther north, the North Bay and District Health Unit has not had the same staff problem. Because the cottage population is less dense and the cottages newer than those in Muskoka, four inspectors find they can visit all construction sites — provided the health unit is advised that a building permit has been issued.

Thomas Elliott, the unit's chief public health inspector, says both municipal councils and the public in general are becoming more co-operative as interest in pollution problems heightens.

"For the first time a lot of people are actually calling us for advice before they make changes," he said. "People want to know why, and that's nice. They used to regard us just as a sort of police force."

Although the unit gets 600 or 700 complaints a summer of evident pollution sources in cottage areas, the offending cottagers usually are eager to correct the situation, he said. "The result is that, generally speaking, police action doesn't seem to be necessary."

He said the unit has threatened court action against a few polluters but has never had to carry out the threat. "We have had to condemn some buildings, mainly squatters' shacks along the Mattawa River that are carryovers from logging days."

Although most local health authorities are staunch defenders of a properly functioning septic tank as the best sewage treatment system available for rural areas, there are exceptions. One of them is North Bay's medical officer of health, Dr. P. S. deGrosbois, who says septic systems are particularly vulnerable to shifts in earth or vehicular traffic. "They also require maintenance which the public is rarely inclined to give them."

Dr. deGrosbois feels senior levels of government should be doing much more research into possible alternatives. One that fascinates him is the use of extreme heat, perhaps through an atomic-powered toilet that would vaporize wastes.

"There have been experiments with the use of electric toilets but they generally aren't hot enough to get rid of the wastes without a lot of odor," he said.

He said the only research he knows of in Canada was conducted by the army, which a few years ago devised an atomic "hotplate" for use in Arctic areas where conventional sewage disposal systems cannot deal with permafrost.

He said another possibility that might be studied is a cheap, practical way of separating sewage from water. "Wastes from the typical cottage are 98 percent water and only two percent sewage."

Dr. deGrosbois and Dr. Bennett see little advantage in chemical and limited-flush toilets which are sold as pollution preventers.

"Partial systems are no answer," Dr. Bennett said, pointing out that in most instances cottagers who install them continue diverting kitchen and laundry wastes from the septic tanks. "A lot of people think everything that doesn't come from the bowels isn't sewage."

Supervision of cottage sewage systems in the Haliburton and Kawartha lakes is divided between the Peterborough City-County Health Unit and the Haliburton, Kawartha, Pine Ridge District Health Unit.

(Provincial authorities who would like to see the two authorities merged have denied the Peterborough unit the 75-percent grant support provided the district unit. However, the health board in Peterborough has decided a regional unit would end up costing more and lowering the present high level of services.)

The Peterborough unit is better staffed than its neighbor with a total of eight public health inspectors on staff for the one county. The four-county district unit has 10 inspectors, only five of whom are based in cottage areas.

The district unit is headed by Dr. Charlotte Horner, who 25 years ago became Ontario's first full-time woman MOH when she organized public health services in Northumberland County. She was appointed director of the Northumberland-Durham Health Unit in 1952 and continued in the position until the district unit was formed last year.

Dr. Horner says the unit tries to make pre-construction site inspections "but Whiterock Estates has been an awful problem for us." The widely advertised Whiterock developments have been mainly outside the cottage areas but sales of the 10-acre lots have been on such a scale that the job of inspecting the lots has been immense.

"Whiterock says it will give the money back to the purchasers if they are unable to get building permits and the councils now require us to give clearances. Unfortunately this has meant we can't provide pre-construction inspections of all lots elsewhere in the district," Dr. Horner said.

Dr. R. C. Wade, MOH at Peterborough since 1966, feels there no longer is such a thing as a "cottage" in his county. Most of them are summer homes and a lot are being used the year round.

Dr. Wade says ideally cottages would not be permitted in Shield areas. But if there must be such development it should be based on the use of holding tanks. "It's hard to get fill for a tile bed in the Precambrian Shield and in some cases you can't get the fill to the site."

The MOH cited the case of Coon Lake in Burleigh Township. A few years ago the Lands and Forests Department sought the health unit's approval of a proposal to subdivide Crown land along the lake's rocky shoreline.

The approval was given, subject to the limitation that sewage disposal must be by pit privy.

An auction of the lots wasn't conducted until this spring, by which time the Peterborough health unit was no longer approving cottage lots which were unsuitable for septic tanks.

As a result, purchasers are suddenly discovering that they cannot build on the lots and complaints are reaching both the health unit and Queen's Park. Dr. Wade suggested the probable outcome will be an offer by Lands and Forests to buy back the land at the sale price.

NOISE:
POLLUTING THE ENVIRONMENT

Barbara J. Culliton

Arthur Conan Doyle once described Sherlock Holmes plucking his violin for a fly trapped under an upturned tumbler. Holmes's experiment, to observe the effects of sound on a living organism, has a powerful analogy in the modern world. We are all flies, trapped among the noisy resonances of industrialized society. And whether Holmes understood or only suspected it, sound does have an effect on living creatures.

Like a drug that produces measurable effects when it enters the body, noise is being found to induce physiological changes that are suspected of having a relation to disease.

"Noise is a stress, an environmental pollutant, an insult," says Dr. Chauncey Leake of the University of California Medical Center at San Francisco. "It affects the nervous, endocrine and reproductive system. It may damage unborn children."

According to Dr. Bruce Welch of the Friends of Psychiatric Research in Baltimore, "The physiological effects of sound are measurable at as low as 70 decibels. They are all-pervasive, most threatening to the young and yet difficult to spell out in man because problems arise from long-term, chronic exposure." Dr. Welch was chairman of a three-day symposium on the physiological effects of sound at the recent

meeting of the American Association for the Advancement of Science in Boston.

Says Dr. Samuel Rosen, "Any loud noise, whether we like it or not, constricts blood vessels. Eventually, this could cause permanent damage." In addition to constricted vessels, says Dr. Rosen, a consulting physician at the New York Eye and Ear Infirmary and the Mount Sinai School of Medicine, there are other physiological reactions to noise: The skin pales, pupils dilate, eyes close and the voluntary and involuntary muscles tense. Gastric secretions diminish and adrenalin is suddenly injected into the blood stream.

"These changes," says Dr. Rosen, "occur via the vegetative nervous system, which plays a role in regulating the changing caliber of blood vessels." Constriction occurs irrespective of whether an individual likes or dislikes a given noise. And it occurs regardless of whether a person has been exposed to that sound in the past. However, the severity of response appears to be clearly related to some degree to prior exposure and to an individual's general state of health and life style.

Dr. Rosen and his colleagues have conducted comparative studies on the effects of noise on urban dwellers in the German city of Dortmund, on New

Yorkers and on the primitive Mabaans, an African tribe living in southeast Sudan. The urbanites came from an environment in which loud noise is commonplace. Their diets were rich in meat, butter and other animals fats. Coronary disease and hypertension are not uncommon among them. The Mabaans, on the other hand, live in virtual silence, are mainly vegetarians and rarely, if ever, have high blood pressure.

When exposed to noise at 90 and 95 decibels, the noise level of a heavy truck, blood vessels constricted both in primitive tribesmen and individuals from industrial societies. Among tribesmen, however, constriction and relaxation of vessels were rapid, showing both quick response to and quick recovery from the stress of sound. Among the Westerners, vessels remained constricted for longer periods, indicating a lesser degree of elasticity in their blood vessels and a diminished capacity to recover from the effects of noise.

"If there is already present somatic disease like atherosclerosis or coronary heart disease, continued noise exposure could endanger health and aggravate the pathology by adding insult to injury," Dr. Rosen suggests.

Noise, in experimental animals at least, also affects kidney function through its action on hormones. In 1964, Australian pharmacologist Dr. Mary F. Lockett was conducting tests on endocrine activity in rats when a violent thunderstorm occurred in Perth. "The next morning," she recounts, "the animals were badly out of salt and water balance." Subsequently, she exposed the rats to recorded thunderclaps of 100 decibels at a low frequency of 150 cycles per second. The noise stimulated the release of a hormone, oxytocin, from the pituitary gland. Oxytocin, in turn, stimulated the kidney, resulting in enhanced excretion of salt and water. High-frequency sounds had another effect. They stimulated adrenalin secretion up to 20 times normal levels and caused water retention, rather than excretion, because adrenalin inhibits synthesis of antidiuretic hormone, which inhibits the excretion of fluids.

Dr. John L. Fuller of the Jackson Laboratories in Bar Harbor, Me., sees animals' response to noise as a valuable laboratory model for studying the biology of stress and the chemistry of the brain as it affects the nervous system. With Dr. Robert L. Collins, he has been looking at sound-induced seizures in inbred strains of mice. The genetic makeup of a mouse influences its response to noise. "Not all strains will convulse when stimulated by sound," Dr. Fuller explains, "but some are clearly more susceptible than others."

However, though genes play a role in this mouse syndrome, which has no exact counterpart in human medicine (except for rare cases of musicogenic epilepsy), Dr. Fuller has shown that environmental stress at the right time can convert a theoretically unsusceptible mouse into a convulsive one. If a mouse from a genetically resistant strain is subjected to loud sounds — 95 decibels or more — on about the sixteenth day of life, subsequent noises will drive it into convulsions.

"Roughly speaking," Dr. Fuller comments, "16 days in a mouse's life are equivalent to between two and four years in a child's life. There is no direct evidence that noise actually harms human young, but the effects of sound are insidious and not easily detectable. While there is no reason to believe it causes seizures in man, sound could be related to behaviour — to aggression or passivity." Genetically resistant strains of mice stressed by noise at an older age generally do not become convulsive.

Decibels		
Large Pneumatic Riveter (3")	125+	Boiler Shop (Maximum Level)
Rock and Roll Band (peak)	120	
Overhead Jet Aircraft (500')	115+	
Loud Motorcycle	110	
Construction Noise (Hammers and Compressors) (10')	110	
Loud Outboard Motor	102	
Subway Train (20')	95+	
Train Whistles (500')	90+	
Heavy Truck (25')	90+	
	40+	Average Residence
	*32	Room in a Quiet London Dwelling (at Midnight)

*"A" Scale, a modified form of decibel, weighted to emphasize the upper frequencies. All other figures are in the flat or "C" scale.
Compiled by Citizens for a Quieter City, Inc. from government documents, 1969.

A scale of threatening sounds from trucks to riveters.

In spite of the fact that researchers have yet to accumulate all of the data on the subject they would like, they agree that it is reasonable to postulate that the greatest threat is to unborn and very young children. Presumably, the developing fetus, whose organs and tissues are taking form, is the most sensitive of biological systems. Sound constricting a mother's blood vessels could certainly take its toll on an unborn child.

According to Dr. William Geber of the University of Georgia School of Medicine in Augusta, decreased blood flow in the uterine and placental vessels probably results in varying degrees of disruption of the normal interchange of oxygen, carbon dioxide, nutrients and waste products between maternal and fetal tissues. Therefore, it is possible to create permanently both gross anatomical abnormalities and more subtle deviations in such diverse systems as brain function or metabolic pathways.

To eliminate the potentially adverse effects of noise, prevention appears to be the only certain, but obviously elusive, method. Drug studies, however, indicate there is one experimental compound that acts to reduce the effects of loud sounds, though it is of interest primarily as a tool for approaching biological investigations, not as a general prophylactic.

Surprisingly the administration of ordinary tranquilizers such as reserpine and chlorpromazine not only fails to block the stress of noise but actually enhances its physiologic effects, in some cases leading to an animal's death.

Dr. Joseph P. Buckley of the University of Pittsburgh explains that this occurs because of a resulting overstimulation of the adrenal cortex followed by an insufficiency of adrenal hormones.

But he reports that a compound used experimentally in late stages of human hypertension does protect rats from adverse reactions to noise. Alpha-methyl-para-tyrosine decreases brain levels of noradrenalin, a neurotransmitter active in the process of blood vessel constriction, causing a decrease, rather than increase, in blood pressure.

"This compound has been rather unsuccessful in clinical trials involving patients with advanced hypertension," Dr. Buckley observes, "probably because in these cases a clear kidney disorder has developed and become a primary factor in the disease. But alpha-methyl-paratyrosine, it now appears, may be useful in treating patients in early stages of hypertension." The drug has Food and Drug Administration approval for experimental use only.

While certain effects of noise can be observed in man, and while these effects can be more clearly defined in experimental animals in controlled circumstances, it is also apparent that in assessing its effects on man in relation to environmental disease, other factors, including genetics, the general health of the cardiovascular system and routine noise levels, must be considered. Says Dr. Rosen, "To separate these factors is like trying to restore a scrambled egg into a single white and yolk, placed neatly in the original shell."

THE BIG CITY IS THE BEST PLACE TO GET LUNG CANCER

Tom Hazlitt

A provincial government survey shows soaring deaths by lung cancer in the industrial cities of Ontario, and poses the possibility that air pollution is at least partly to blame.

The study, directed by the environmental health branch of the provincial health department, is part of a continuing effort to identify and isolate the "kill factor" in big city living.

Preliminary results show that there are up to 40 percent more deaths by lung cancer among city-dwelling males than among men of the same age living in rural districts. There is also a differential of about 30 percent between residents of industrial cities like Toronto and Hamilton, and non-industrial cities like Ottawa and London, Ont.

Until now, available statistics have shown only a rising incidence of fatal lung cancer in the province as a whole, part of a world-wide development generally blamed on cigarette smoking.

The current survey, directed by the health department's Dr. R. B. Sutherland, represents the first attempt to check back on death certificates and other documents to determine where

Reprinted with permission *Toronto Daily Star,* January 17, 1970.

the victims lived and what conditions they might have encountered during their lives.

Sutherland, chief of the studies service of the environmental health branch, has compiled figures showing 20 causes of death in 20 major centres, reaching back to the census of 1956.

Fed into computer

The mass of material must now be analyzed in detail, but trends for lung cancer mortality can readily be picked out.

They show this disturbing picture:

In Toronto the male death rate from lung cancer is 27 percent above the provincial average. In industrial Hamilton, the male death rate is 46 percent above average.

But in non-industrial London, Ont., the rate is only 3 percent above normal and in Ottawa 5 percent.

The differentials are well beyond the statistical threshold that could be attributed to chance.

Practical difficulties in obtaining documents make it almost impossible to obtain a precise death rate for rural Ontario. But if London and Ottawa are near the bottom of the industrial scale, and the death rates there are near or slightly above average, it follows by simple arithmetic that the rural rate must be much lower than the average, since all industrial rates are higher than the average.

Sutherland and his co-workers are attempting now to establish a pattern of lung cancer deaths from the total remaining when deaths in the 20 main cities are subtracted.

The provincial survey will be subject to close scrutiny when published and presented to the scientific community.

But a preliminary study shows three possibilities:

1) Existing air pollution levels as set out in provincial legislation may not be providing the protection expected of them.

2) Cigarette smoking, while undoubtedly a danger, may not tell the whole story about lung cancer.

3) There may in fact be a "multiplication factor" involving smoking and smoking in a polluted atmosphere.

Major defect

A major defect in the provincial government study is that the smoking history of lung cancer victims is not known.

But there is nothing except conventional wisdom to suggest that city dwellers smoke significantly more than rural residents. And there is no reason to suppose the residents of Hamilton smoke more than people who live in Ottawa.

Sutherland, who works closely with provincial air pollution officials, does not make an outright claim that air pollution is to blame for the "rather sharp" differentials which he has discovered.

"But something is causing people to die in the industrial cities of lung cancer," he said.

"Certainly, the figures to date suggest that air pollution plays a part. They also suggest that non-smokers are feeling some effect from pollution, and that there may be a synergistic relationship between smoking and air pollution."

(A synergistic relationship implies a multiplying factor between two ingredients, so that the total impact of a combination of two conditions is more than the total of each independently.)

Big trouble

The theory that smoking in association with air pollution equals big medical trouble receives backing from a joint U.S.-Canadian study conducted last year in heavily polluted St. Louis and relatively "clean" Winnipeg.

That study found that emphysema, a fast-growing lung disease often blamed on smoking, was far more prevalent in St. Louis than in Winnipeg.

The U.S.-Canadian study was able to record the smoking habits of its subjects, and it found that emphysema among matched groups of smokers was four times higher in St. Louis than in Winnipeg.

Reporting in the Archives of Environmental Health, the authors said that a synergistic relationship between pollution and smoking must be considered.

Sutherland, a veteran of environmental medicine, used to smoke between two and three packages of cigarettes daily. Now he doesn't smoke at all.

He explained how he and his colleagues started out almost from scratch in their attempt to scrutinize causes of death by geographical place of residence.

First it was necessary to establish a fatality rate for each cause of death, by comparing actual deaths throughout the province with actual census counts in the areas concerned, and breaking these down into five-year age groups.

They found that the rate for male lung cancer has increased roughly five times since 1931 in the age group between 45 and 54, and 20 times in the group over 75.

In the past, statisticians have been unable to relate this increase to geographical areas, partly because people tend to seek treatment and eventually die in the major centres.

Sutherland and crew went back to the death certificates to record actual places of residence.

When analyzed by computer, the massive array of facts and figures should provide the first factual picture of death — where, why and when — in relation to the environment.

Even the preliminary figures show that while residents of big cities die of lung cancer at far more than the average rate, fewer than average city residents die in automobile accidents.

Sutherland says he assumes that is because rural people are more often exposed to high speed highway driving.

Eventually, Sutherland expects to explore patterns between all cases of abnormal mortality and environmental peculiarities. This would include checking geographical sub-areas, such as specific sections of Toronto, against known sources of air pollution.

Perhaps the most disturbing aspect of the lung cancer findings lies in the shadow they throw on the effectiveness of existing regulations on air pollution.

The regulations are designed to keep the air over Toronto, and elsewhere, at a level thought to be safe.

But if the air is safe, what causes increased lung cancer, for smokers and non-smokers?

The main pollutants in Toronto are sulphur dioxide, suspended particulates (smoke), oxidants, oxides of nitrogen, and carbon monoxide — the last three of which come chiefly from automobiles.

With the exception of sulphur dioxide, provincial government measuring devices in the Metro area show readings well below the "safe" levels.

The legal level of sulphur dioxide emissions, largely due to industrial and residential furnaces, is set at a 24-hour average of one-tenth part per million parts of air. In January, the peak month, the level often climbs to .11 and .17 parts per million. And the annual average, set at .02 parts per million, worked out to .07 last year.

Such a level is nevertheless well

below what might be considered dangerous, according to provincial authorities.

But the chief difficulty in setting air pollution criteria appears to be that so-called "safe" levels have been set over the years at some fraction of the level used as a maximum for healthy men in industry.

Nothing, or almost nothing, is known about the accumulative effect of a lifetime of inhaling polluted air at low levels.

Nothing, or almost nothing, is known about the effect of such low levels on infants or adults with bronchial troubles.

And very little is known about the impact of a combination of pollutants, such as is found in Toronto.

For example, hydro-carbons and nitrogen oxides combine in the presence of sunlight and still air to form occidents, the ingredient of infamous Los Angeles smog which causes headaches and eye irritation.

Largely due to lack of sunshine, ozone is found in Toronto in amounts ranging from zero to only about half the acceptable level.

But that doesn't mean to say that climatic conditions peculiar to Toronto or some other Canadian city don't start off a chain reaction of their own.

One theory is that combinations of sulphur dioxide; and the suspended particulates in smoke are more dangerous than either one by itself.

The reasoning is that particulates are largely carbon. Carbon has the power to "soak up" noxious gases including sulphur dioxide.

Thus a person inhaling particulates into his lungs may also ingest quantities of sulphur dioxide much greater than that found in the atmosphere generally.

Pollution and the legal levels

The Air Pollution Control Act (1967) sets criteria for most pollutants in the air over Ontario. Here is a summary of the levels as set by law, the average conditions in mid-town Toronto, and the extremes recorded from time to time:

POLLUTANT	PRESCRIBED LEVEL	AVERAGE LEVEL	EXTREME
Sulphur Dioxide	.02 ppm	.07 ppm	.17 ppm
Oxidants	.07 ppm	.03 ppm	.06 ppm
Nitrogen Dioxide	.10 ppm	.04 ppm	.22 ppm
Carbon Monoxide	15 ppm	3 ppm	15 ppm

*ppm indicates parts of pollutant per one million parts air by volume.

WASHDAY CAN PUT SPARKLE BACK INTO WATER

Stu Brooks

Stu Brooks is a staff reporter for the Hamilton Spectator.

Women refuse to be soft-soaped about lake water pollution.

And if they demand low-phosphate detergents they will get them, say Hamilton chain store managers, and their views are buttressed by rising sales of low-phosphate washing products.

At least one of Ontario's three large detergent makers, Procter and Gamble Co. of Canada Ltd., agrees that the consumer will have the final say in the phosphate controversy.

With the issue coming to a boil, a Toronto firm has added fuel to the fire by marketing a phosphate-free detergent through Mac's Milk Ltd., five of whose outlets are in Hamilton. And by April 6 they hope their Crown detergent will be in all stores, says detergent company president, Bill Phelan.

The company, Canadian Floor Service Ltd., had their detergent tested by the Ontario Water Resources Commission who found no significant amount of phosphate nutrients in it.

When the family wash is done with such detergents and waste water reaches Lake Ontario it will not kill desirable underwater life. Nor will it nourish algae, sludgeworms, bloodworms and other pollution-tolerant bacteria that wading youngsters at the beach can happily do without.

So great is the concentration of phosphorous compounds in Lake Ontario that it (and Lake Erie) is in "an advanced state of eutrophication," says a recent study by the U.S. department of the interior. It means the dense growth of plant life decays and robs the water of oxygen, especially in summer.

Lake Ontario, in fact, is close to dying just as the countryside bursts into life this Easter.

Cold water is thrown on the Toronto sales venture by the three large detergent makers, Procter and Gamble, Colgate-Palmolive Ltd., and Lever Detergents Ltd.

A body representing them — the water quality committee — sums up their philosophy.

"The three companies are opposed to any reduction in phosphates for two reasons," says a spokesman. "It would mess up their product which would not work as well. And the phosphate reduction would not accomplish anything."

The spokesman says it would accomplish nothing, mainly because almost

Reprinted with permission of *The Hamilton Spectator,* March 30, 1970, by Stu Brooks.

twice as much phosphorus per person each year is used in detergents in the United States compared with Canada. There is much more pollution of Lakes Ontario and Erie from the U.S.A. side not only because of that factor but due to the few numbers of American sewage plants despite a higher lakeside population, he said.

The water quality committee sends out literature giving the Canadian detergent industry's viewpoints. It explains the constant research being done by the industry's own laboratories and points out that in Dec. 1966 it voluntarily cured the detergent foam on lakes, rivers and streams of which people complained.

The committee's literature agrees that phosphorus is an important factor in quickening a lake's plant growth and diminishing the vital oxygen.

"In its final death phase the lake will completely fill with sediment and become a bog or a swamp and eventually a meadow," says a section on eutrophication.

But any legislation requiring removal of phosphates (phosphorus-based materials) from detergents would be unrealistic and scientifically unsound claims the committee.

"It would create a major cleaning problem in Canada by removing from supermarkets and grocery stores the familiar detergent products vital to the housewife for the machine laundering, automatic dishwashing, and household cleaning."

A phosphate ban in detergents would set back cleanliness standards by 20 years and housewives would find it virtually impossible to continue to enjoy the benefits of the modern automatic clothes washing machine, says the committee.

"All washing appliances used in the home and restaurants are programmed for these products (detergents). And the automatic dishwasher would become useless since highly specialized phosphate-containing detergents are also essential in this application," claims the literature.

Washing machine manufacturers were incredulous when asked about the statement's suggested fate of their machines if phosphate-free detergents become the vogue.

"The statement does not hold water and I cannot believe it to be true," said the service manager for all-Canada of a major washing machine manufacturer. "Phosphates simply contribute to the washing ability of the detergent, keeping the dirt in suspension for a longer period of time."

Of the non-phosphate detergent being marketed by Canadian Floor Service, the service manager said this undoubtedly has now been used in many washers and the type of soap used cannot be a determining factor.

Certain companies pack a particular brand of detergent in their new washer but this does not necessarily mean the brand is recommended for that machine, he says. The sales divisions from the various brands of detergent take it in turn to provide free samples from their budgets.

There is more selectivity with modern washing machines but basically the principle is the same as in the 1940s. Now, as then, machines are not designed for particular detergents with or without phosphates, says the service manager.

The service manager with another national company agrees and adds: "I think the detergent industry has got everyone brainwashed to a degree. They spend more money on advertising than anyone else."

Both service managers concede the water quality committee's views ring truer when it comes to dishwashers, although they use far less detergent than clothes washing machines.

The detergent makers have one Canadian source of phosphate compound, the Electric Reduction Company of Canada Ltd., known as Erco.

Energy, Mines and Resources Minister Joe Greene aims for complete elimination of phosphates from detergents by 1972. The Americans are recommending similar measures and a report to the International Joint Commission said complete replacement of phosphorous compounds in detergents should be made "as soon as possible but not later than 1972."

And Erco, the sole manufacturer of tri-sodium-phosphate for detergents and doing a $150 million a year business, is worried.

Erco's manager of patents and information, Robert Cale, presented a brief last week to Parliament's national resources committee.

The phosphate problem will be under federal regulation by Aug. 1 with the highest percentage allowable in detergents likely to be set at 20 percent, compared with the present level of up to 52.5 percent. And Mr. Cale contends that a ban on phosphates will not save Canada's lakes from death.

Mr. Cale's views are generally similar to those of the detergent companies. He points out that Canadian household detergents contribute only five percent of total phosphorus entering the lakes and if existing sewage plants are modernized the contribution would be only one percent of the total.

Instead of the "unrealistic" 1972 deadline for a total ban on phosphates the manager asked the Commons committee to put off any decision until then. This would give his industry more time for study and research.

Mr. Cale says the only serious contender as a replacement of phosphates is NTA, sodium nitriloacetate, but even this needs two years of full tests and proof of safety.

And he says the present total North American production capacity for NTA is under 75,000 tons yearly, whereas 500,000 tons would be needed in the U.S. alone to replace phosphates at a ratio of one pound NTA to 1½ pounds of phosphates.

Even if NTA is fully approved it will need three years to set up new plants of required safety standards, says Mr. Cale.

This forecast contrasts with the optimistic mood at Canadian Floor Service. It employs only 12 full-time and 40 part-time people, operates a cleaning service and makes soap and waxes under the name Crown Chemicals.

Bill Phelan, president, says the formula for his phosphate-free detergent is his company's own and could be something like NTA.

The first 20-ounce boxes at 53 cents went like hotcakes in Mac's Milk Ltd. stores and in the first three weeks Mr. Phelan went on to five-pound plastic bags and tentatively ordered 100,000 but quickly increased the order to 250,000.

The five-pound bags are expected to retail in Hamilton at $1.59.

Mr. Phelan says the Ontario Water Resources Commission finalized their report on his product recently and came up with less than one percent phosphate content.

Mr. Phelan says he is amazed at housewives' interest in pollution.

"We are getting many phone calls from them and it is they who will make or break our venture," he says. Most housewives are impressed by the fact that a small firm has done something while the "giants" are still talking about it and spending thousands of dollars to show it can't be done, says Mr. Phelan.

It took his partner, chemical engineer Nelson Chu, only one week to come up

with the solution. And Mr. Phelan laughs at the big detergent companies' comments that "it can't be done so quickly" and "it's very expensive to research."

"We have left the verdict to housewives and they are completley satisfied. We not only can do it but have done it and it's on the market," says the confident businessman.

Meantime the chain stores in Hamilton have noticed the trend towards lower-phosphate detergents and have increased their orders in recent weeks.

And most of them display notices near detergents showing how much phosphate each brand has. The notices are reproductions of a Spectator chart of Feb. 9, based on information by Pollution Probe at the University of Toronto.

In some stores the notices were not conspicuous. But at Food City, on Queenston Road, a large two-foot square notice hung from the ceiling above the detergents. And the checkout girl put a smaller notice in each customer's bag of purchases.

One store reported a 50 percent increase in sales of Wisk, with only 10.5 percent phosphates, in recent weeks. And the Ivory Snow sales of soap flakes had risen from a case in six weeks to two cases in one week, with similar increases for other brands. The price has not changed.

About half of the women shoppers questioned in five stores were not concerned about phosphate and many of them did not understand the issue of pollution. A young assistant supervisor says she is sure that many women customers think wrongly it is the manufacturing of detegents itself that pollutes the water. She believes there should be more explanation on television and in newspapers that it is what goes down the kitchen sink and drains that helps to pollute lakes and streams.

Around 25 percent of shoppers say they simply buy the detergent that does most good at the most suitable price, with no thought of phosphates. The remaining 25 percent included some with strong views about detergents and pollution.

Mrs. Eileen Lamb, of Braemar Place, asked specially where Wisk was and later revealed that she carries around with her a copy of the Pollution Probe chart in her purse.

"I find many of my friends are doing the same thing and eight of us were talking about it at luncheon yesterday. We shop around for the low-phosphate detergents and see which of them gives the better wash. I am very concerned about pollution of the lakes and I hope more stores will advertise as this one does."

And although the individual store managers had to leave comment to head office they all say one thing: "It's up to the customers in the end. Whatever they want — will be on the shelves for them."

Some of this awareness of public concern is due to the activities of CHOP (Clear Hamilton of Pollution) members at McMaster University. Helped by high school students they have quietly questioned shoppers at many of the main stores on Saturdays.

They find that more people are becoming conscious of pollution and aware of its undesirable consequences.

OF MUCK AND MEN

"If current trends continue, the future of life on earth could be endangered." Nothing to do with the risk of nuclear war. The quotation is from a sober 60-page report published in June by the United Nations secretary-general, after the member governments had unanimously agreed to confer about the things man is doing to his environment by "air and water pollution, erosion and other forms of soil deterioration, secondary effects of biocides, waste and noise." A very similar apocalyptic theme has marked the series of Reith lectures just broadcast in Britain by Dr. Frank Fraser Darling.

Mark Twain complained that everybody talked about the weather, but nobody did anything about it. With the environment as a whole we now seem to be doing a bit better than that. You might even say that something encouragingly like a constructive panic is on. The Council of Europe has just launched its European Conservation Year, and Nato's new Committee on the Challenges of Modern Society has held its first meeting. The Un Assembly has approved plans for a major conference. In Britain the Prime Minister announced last week that a standing royal commission on environmental pollution is to be set up, and that a watchdog group of scientists will be appointed by Mr. Crosland, the minister in general charge of these matters.

This is all very impressive, but one is left with the fear that the massed ranks now setting out to do battle against the pale horsemen of this new apocalypse may end up trampling one another to death. Now that it is legitimate to be against motherhood, "environment" looks like becoming a battle-cry that will be both unchallengeable and universally fashionable. Everybody is in on the act. Unfortunately, some of the new enthusiasm seems to spring from mixed motives.

Suspicions of this kind have surrounded the new Nato initiative, which was stimulated by President Nixon. One of his advisers, Mr. Patrick Moynihan, has played a conspicuous part in selling the idea to a dubious North Atlantic Council. Mr. Moynihan, the author of "Maximum Feasible Misunderstanding," has been leaning rather heavily on such suggestions as that, by the year 2000, the level of the oceans could rise by ten feet as a result of the increased carbon dioxide content of the atmosphere. This content has, indeed, already been increased by 10 percent by the use of coal and oil fuels (each transatlantic airliner puts a hundred tons of carbon dioxide into the atmosphere); and the restoration of the balance by photosynthesis in plant life on land and in the sea may be increasingly jeopardised by human spoliation of the environment. But

Reprinted with permission of *The Economist,* December 20, 1969.

55

scientists have been unable to agree in predicting the long-term effects of a fouler atmosphere on the earth's surface temperature, and hence on the sea level.

What is agreed is that we are destabilising the balance of nature in this and other ways, and that where remedies are available they will mostly require action on an international scale. For this action, however, a military alliance seems a curious agent. It is understandable that a bid should be made to improve Nato's image by bringing it into the business. But it would be a bad setback if this kind of public relations activity were to interfere with the urgent job of mounting the necessary international effort in the proper way. Very sensibly, the Swedish initiators of the current plan for a UN conference have emphasised that the last thing they want is to bring into being any more organisations, or to inhibit the work already being done by existing ones; on the contrary, the idea is to encourage that work. Their plan, which has been broadly accepted, is to use the approach of the conference to stimulate action and then to make the actual meeting a brisk, eye-catching affair of no more than two weeks.

They have had the satisfaction of drawing a positive response from the Russians, whose representative at the UN set dogma aside and conceded that the impairment of air, water and soil was a problem that was neither automatically resolved by communism nor incurable under capitalism. In both political systems the lesson is being painfully learned that, apart from the fact that some of the damage is irreversible, the cost of repairing damage already done is usually much higher than the cost of prevention would have been. (Yet the Russians, with the hideous example of the north American Great Lakes before their eyes, have recently begun to pollute Lake Baikal.) Even more slowly, it is being realised that the whole process is accelerating. The mess we are making now could have catastrophic effects not upon a distant posterity — assuming that there is going to be any such thing — but within a few decades.

The achievements that shine like bright deeds in a filthy world are mainly local ones. Coal-fire smog has gone from London, mercury poisoning from Sweden's lakes. The Ruhr is being cleaned up; Britain's bird population is reviving; the advance of the man-made deserts is being checked at many points. But air and water continue to carry pollutants across frontiers and indeed across the globe. The agreement reached in Brussels last month on pollution from oil tankers is so far the only general international instrument that bears directly on the problem. The need to shape a wide and effective range of such instruments is the more obvious in view of the blunt fact that no nation will readily foot a bill for preventing its muck from reaching its neighbours unless it gets matching assurances from other nations.

In the UN Assembly a few weeks ago, full support for the Swedish conference project was voiced by an American delegate, who happened to be Mrs. Shirley Temple Black, and who puzzled but pleased fellow delegates with such statements as: "In many ways we have created a thorny bed. None of us wants it. We have come to a point of many turnings." Before we are through with the environment thing (assuming it doesn't get through with us first), we are going to be exposed to a lot of verbiage much more baffling than that; but even the foggiest words are a less alarming additive to the atmosphere than an excess of carbon dioxide. For one forceful exposition of what it is all about, those who did not hear Dr. Fraser Darling's lectures might well read them in the *Listener* or in book form; for another, they may be referred to a remarkable book* which was originally published in Sweden three years ago and which is credited with having inspired the subsequent Swedish drive to bring the whole problem to the forefront of international discussion. Some day we may all have cause for gratitude to these prophets of avoidable doom.

* "On the Shred of a Cloud." By Rolf Edberg. *University of Alabama Press.* 200 pages. $6.50.

FAREWELL MY LOVE
THE CAR

Oliver Clausen

Oliver Clausen, a former editor of the Globe Magazine, is a frequent contributor to Canadian periodicals.

Few Torontonians thought about it that way back in August 1967 — it was a time when they were still titillated by those types and now the types were making news by sitting-in on Yorkville Avenue in a bid to have it barred to motor traffic — but it looks increasingly now as if Toronto was getting a foretaste of much more spectacular things to come. Not in that city alone or even necessarily, but throughout the modern world where the monster that is the private automobile is day by day killing the cities and life itself.

The car, from being love object and status symbol and all that, is rapidly turning into a society-rending *issue*. Already, characteristically, young radicals are railing against it as the very symbol of inhuman North American civilization (though automania is just as bad elsewhere, including the Communist countries where ordinary people must be content to *dream* about owning a car). But the revulsion extends much further — citizens' protests have led to the halting of expressway projects in 16 U.S. cities — to the point where it is now possible to discern a gathering wholesale revolt.

It was a limited enough little issue in Yorkville: the long-haired young just wanted to be left alone on *their* quaint street, alone from the interminable procession of cars filled with suburbanites gawking as if in a zoo. They had a good enough point for that matter, unacceptable as their arrogant confrontation tactics were, for Yorkville is exactly the sort of neighborhood in any city that should be for pedestrians only.

But that was 31 long months ago, 31 intensely important months during which mankind has awakened to more vital stuff than hippies' demands to do their own thing. Stuff like man's own impending extinction if he carries on as now. Stuff like the prospect that the sunlight reaching earth will be reduced

Reprinted by permission from *The Globe Magazine,* March 7, 1970.

58

by half by 1985, that the world will die by century's end. Largely because of the car.

There isn't room for its recklessly proliferating breed, not if there is to be room for the good life. It spews nearly 100 million tons of pollutants into the North American air annually, turning our streets into open sewers.

Is it possible to be motorized and at the same time civilized? The question is posed by a U.S. transportation expert, Wilfred Owen of the Brookings Institution. It's getting harder to answer in the affirmative. Is it civilization if we have to wear gas masks to survive in the cities in another 10 years or so? If school children, day after day, are ordered not to exercise so they won't breathe too deep draughts of air that is really ambient filth — as is happening in Los Angeles right now?

The car causes as much as 80 percent of the air pollution that is suffocating the cities, as well as 75 percent of the noise pollution. A couple of other automotive pollutants: 8 million cars junked annually in North America, 105 million tires. Think of the giant tankers that split open, their oil (as much as 75 million gallons in one ship) destroying the ocean before being turned into gasoline to destroy the air.

One understands the odd ceremony that took place at San Jose State College in California the other day. A group of students bought a 1970 Ford Maverick (nice little car, by the way). They began to push it along so as not to foul the atmosphere, but agreed to have it towed on police orders. Then they lowered it into a deep grave and threw soil on top. RIP car, and may you never rise.

Closer to home, in Toronto, yet another consequence of automania has set citizen against citizen in a remarkable socio-ideological battle at times reminiscent of civil war — verbal, so far. Can anything since the issue of wet versus dry have polarized the community as has the spectre of that massive slab of concrete, the Spadina Expressway, poised like a cobra to strike at the heart of the city? What else, even in this age of violent expressions, has created such enmity?

Between suburbia and downtown in this case, between the outer city and the inner core. The issue is really quite simple as I perceive it: must Toronto proper be turned into a polluted wasteland of concrete and automotive steel so the people from the dreary suburbs can more conveniently drive to work? It is hard to see the Spadina Expressway being pushed through without encountering physical violence.

And the car is responsible for the garish vulgarity of billboards and drive-ins along the access routes into the city. It kills more than 5,000 Canadians a year. It plays havoc with family economies; most car owners can't really afford to be.

Dr. Gordon M. Shrum, chairman of British Columbia Hydro: "The first country to abolish the car will be the healthiest, happiest and wealthiest in the world.

Yeah. There were 4.3 million cars registered in Canada in 1961. There will be 7 million this year. The way it's going, that number will nearly double by the end of the decade.

But can we allow it to? Specifically and of prime urgency, can we allow the automobile to retain the upper hand over *people* in the city? With our sudden and long overdue concern for the environment that sustains life on earth — and with the quality of that life — this now seems bound to be a gut issue of the Seventies.

Not that I am against cars. Only against what they do and represent. I don't own one any more, figuring that the urbane life surely is in town and preferably within subway reach of work, but I enjoy driving in a way that surprisingly few car owners seem to do. Last summer, while preparing a special Globe Magazine issue on the automobile, I tried out 15 cars from seven different countries and again had to conclude that there are few pleasures — perhaps only one — more scintillating than aiming an Alfa Romeo Spider Veloce or an E-type Jaguar down a winding country road and just let go.

But those were sports cars, driven for fun on an open road, and hardly relevant to the issue of the automobile as the city's enemy No. 1. I drove others, though. The most enjoyable was the odd-ball Renault 16, but the most memorable a big bloated air conditioned Cadillac on one of those insufferably muggy days we had last June. And there, carried to the Caddy extreme, was a clue to why the automobile still holds the upper hand and is such an intractable enemy.

It was just plush transportation, too unwieldy and sluggish-handling to be fun to drive. But you sat there in spacious, silent, air conditioned comfort while all around the poor pedestrian yokels were sweltering and cursing. That's why it's so hard to get at even the more humdrum car. The drive to work is the only chance the average man has to be a private and seemingly complete person, bigger than he really is because he has all that power under his control. I think it's that psychological factor, the ego-building, as much as convenience — often doubtful, with those parking problems — that makes the car in commuter traffic so difficult to stamp out. If it's ever to be done — as it obviously must be — it will call for a revolution in our way of life the more transcendental because it must be against our own selves.

The prime feature of the debate now gathering strength is that objective people — save perhaps some suburbanites who don't care about the city anyway — seem agreed in principle that the car is a socially Bad Thing, yet individually insist on driving and even clamor for freeways. Selfish he is, man, and there is little reason to trust that persuasion and noble appeals will change that. What, then?

Valfrid Paulsson, director-general of Sweden's National Environment Protection Board: "We're already thinking of banning vehicular traffic in the centres of towns with more than 100,000 people." Others advocate prohibitive parking fees.

Force, then, in society's self-defense. But is there no other way? Devices are being introduced that will cut carbon monoxide pollution sharply, but in doing so they require increased engine heat which in turn creates poisonous nitrogen oxide emissions — and with more and more cars in the streets all the time, we'll be anything but better off. Electric or steam engines? But that still wouldn't create *room* for the cars. Smaller, nimbler cars instead of the grotesque mastodons that clog North American streets? Would do no harm — but I have seen much worse traffic jams in small-car Japan and Europe.

In any case, the rising demand is so evidently to reclaim the city for people, wresting it from the automobile. The only key is public transit, and how laggard North Americans have been in that regard. How absurd the sight in our cities of one man driving to work surrounded by a couple of tons of his very own steel, holding up everyone else. It's *he* who has to go somewhere, surely, not his car. An expressway lane can carry no more than 3,000 people an hour in their own cars at the average occupancy rate. A bus lane can transport 30,000, a subway 40,000.

Yet public transit use, such is man's perversity, keeps declining. The Toronto Transit Commission has a hilarious answer to that: if we get fewer passengers, we must cut down on service. So that there you stand an an icy winter's evening, waiting, waiting, waiting for a bus. None comes, you take a cab and decide to drive to work the next day.

The only viable answer, of course, is to improve service, expand transit systems, cut fares, making it so much more convenient and attractive to use public transportation that only the snobs who think there is a social stigma attached to using it will bring their stink boxes to town. Imagine what $220-million of Spadina money could do for public transit. Theodore W. Kheel, a New York transportation expert, puts it this way: "Unless we halt the trend away from mass transporta-tion, this city and most others cannot survive."

Much better public transit, including revolutionary modes not yet in existence, is the carrot. The ban on cars is the stick. Imagine the outcry if it is used. After all, the auto industry in Canada and its direct accessories employ more than 100,000 workers, and they are only some of those directly dependent on the automobile for their living. (And think of the powerful oil industry.)

The cynic may exclaim: What a giant, wasted, nefarious effort they represent! But it can also be noted that the resources are there to be freed for constructive efforts to improve the quality of and indeed, perhaps, to save life.

It could yet be that North America, which inflicted the mass produced automobile on the world, will point the way again by ruling it obsolete.

Part 3

The industrial giants of our continent must accept a great deal of the blame for the environmental pollution we are experiencing. Some corporations are showing a real concern for the damage being done, but society is also at fault for allowing the situation to develop and by demanding a wide variety of products which help to scar our environment. For example, the automobile is notorious for befouling the air. Does the average driver consider himself responsible for this condition? Or even partially responsible? Would he willingly give up the convenience of the automobile to end pollution? If a social policy were proposed to remove a substantial number of automobiles from service in favour of more efficient use of shared space, would he willingly make the necessary economic and social adjustments?

The market demand for attractively or conveniently packaged products has created a special kind of mess. Paper packaging, throwaway pop tins or bottles cannot easily be re-used. What can the corporations do to handle the problems thus created? Are they willing to accept their responsibilities? Are we willing to pay the price?

THE OFFICIAL POLICY OF IMPERIAL OIL LIMITED ON THE CONSERVATION OF THE ENVIRONMENT

Imperial Oil and its employees share the concern of all Canadians for the conservation of the quality of the country's air, water and soil. The company believes that the public interest is best served by regulations that

a) provide the appropriate protection of the environment at the least possible cost to the economy

b) are based on standards for environmental quality developed from adequate data

c) provide reasonable time to develop and implement the methods of control

d) treat equitably all materials and operations that contribute to pollution

e) place control with appropriate governmental agencies

In the field of air, water and soil conservation, it is the company's policy

— to comply with existing regulations

— to provide such additional protection of the environment as is technically feasible and economically practical

— to encourage, support and conduct research to establish standards of quality and to develop and improve methods of measurement and control

— to cooperate with other groups working on protection of the environment, such as universities, control agencies, technical societies and trade associations

— to anticipate future pollution control requirements and to make provision for them in long-range planning

— to keep employees, government officials and the public informed

Reprinted by permission of *The Imperial Oil Review,* December, 1968.

STATEMENT OF ENVIRONMENTAL QUALITY

Henry Ford II

Henry Ford II, the grandson of the founder of the Ford Motor company, is Chairman of the Board of Directors of that company.

I want to discuss today the problem of environmental pollution. I regard this as by far the most important problem facing this Company and the entire industry during the decade ahead.

Today I am publicly committing Ford Motor Company to an intensified effort to minimize pollution from its products and plants in the shortest possible time. There is, of course, no such thing as a completely "clean" motor vehicle or industrial plant, but we will achieve products and manufacturing facilities that do not significantly contaminate our atmosphere, waters or landscape.

I cannot emphasize too strongly my own personal concern and that of Ford Motor Company with removing automobile-related pollutants as a threat to environmental quality. This concern will be reflected not in words but in specific, concrete actions based upon all the scientific, engineering and manufacturing skills at our command.

We are making this commitment because of our recognition that the quality of the environment warrants extraordinary effort on the part of all who may be in a position to improve our physical surroundings. We are able to make this commitment at this time because years of research, development and testing have now brought us to the point where we can foresee, in the near future, the practical achievement of levels of pollution control that seemed out of reach until recently.

Before getting into specifics, let me say that the need for additional progress should not blind anyone to the tremendous progress already made in reducing harmful automotive emissions. Less than two decades ago, very little was known about atmospheric contamination, and it wasn't until 1961 that formal exhaust emission test procedures were adopted in California.

Smog and air pollution are exceedingly complex phenomena and still are not fully understood. Until recently, it was generally assumed that the automobile is responsible for most of the carbon monoxide in the atmosphere and that the lifetime of this pollutant is so long that it might accumulate to a dangerously high level. However, research in our Scientific Laboratory and elsewhere shows that carbon monoxide persists in the atmosphere only about one month before it is dissipated by natural processes. Furthermore, preliminary results indicate that by far the largest part of the carbon monoxide in

Reprinted by permission of The Ford Motor Company, Dearborn, Michigan.

the earth's atmosphere comes from biological sources such as the decay of humus and the metabolism of certain marine animals. The automobile is an important source only in congested urban areas.

Efforts to learn more about the effect of automobile usage on the chemistry of the atmosphere, and also about the effect of atmospheric changes on health and well-being, have been under way for some years in our own laboratories and in conjunction with various oil companies and Federal and California pollution control authorities. We need more of this kind of knowledge in order to establish rational priorities for industry programs and public policy.

In the meantime, however, our own Company and others have taken substantial strides in reducing obnoxious motor vehicle emissions. The various controls we have applied are known to most of you, I'm sure, so I won't go into any detail. But I think it is worth repeating that, in less than a decade, we have reduced the emission of unburned gasoline by more than 80 percent, we have reduced carbon monoxide emissions by almost 70 percent and we start next year to control oxides of nitrogen. This is a major technological accomplishment.

One way to describe this progress is to say that one 1960 car emits as much hydrocarbons as five 1970 cars, and as much carbon monoxide as three 1970 cars.

The peak output of hydrocarbons and carbon monoxide from automobiles in the Los Angeles basin was reached sometime in 1966 — about 1,800 tons of hydrocarbons and more than 9,000 tons of carbon monoxide per day. Neither will ever be that high again, despite increases in the car population, because older cars without emission controls will in time be re-

placed by cars with increasingly effective control equipment.

Apart from its in-house efforts, Ford Motor Company has also been project manager of the Inter-Industry Emission Control program, a three-year cooperative effort to develop an extremely low-emission vehicle. This program was initiated by Ford and Mobil Oil and now includes 11 automobile and oil companies.

The other companies in the IIEC program are: American Oil Company, Atlantic Richfield, Fiat, Marathon Oil, Mitsubishi, Nissan, Standard Oil of Ohio, Sun Oil and Toyo Kogyo.

We are participating in many other such cooperative emission-control studies, but the IIEC program is now at a point where it can demonstrate some tangible results.

Earlier this year, the program achieved its low-emission objectives *in the laboratory* — and I emphasize the experimental or conceptual nature of this work to date. These modifications have now been incorporated into 24 so-called "concept" cars which are being road tested to determine whether or not the emission controls are feasible in terms of durability, operating economy and vehicle performance. The next step will be to explore the adaptation of the most promising of these systems to mass production and their compatibility with service requirements and reasonable cost standards. We have already shared our progress in the IIEC program by sending detailed technical reports to the President's scientific advisor, to the Commissioner of the National Air Pollution Control Administration and to California authorities.

This is only one of the steps we are taking to hasten our work on low-emission vehicles. Where the "state of the art" lags behind public needs and expectations, we will try to push the "state of the art" along faster. Where the cost or performance characteristics of low-emission vehicles fall short of acceptable market standards, we will draw upon every available resource to bring cost and performance into line.

I must emphasize, however, that substantial further reductions of pollution from our products and plants will cost a great deal of money. We believe that the cost of pollution abatement should be regarded as a normal cost of doing business and we recognize that the American people appear to be willing to spend substantially more to improve their environment.

In practice, however, no company can voluntarily assume pollution control costs that are far out of line with those of its competitors. How much should be spent in total to reduce pollution associated with automobiles, and how much reduction should be achieved, are decisions that can be made only by the people acting through their government; they cannot be made by industry acting on its own.

As a manufacturer of motor vehicles, we have a responsibility to develop the lowest-cost ways of meeting whatever standards are set by government. We have an obligation to develop better ways of reducing pollution, even if the costs arc higher. And we have an obligation to help the government develop sound information on the feasibility and the cost of achieving progressively lower levels of pollution.

The government, in turn, has a responsibility to develop standards that will permit the greatest results from the rising national investment in pollution control. It also has the responsibility to decide how much of the nation's income should be spent for this purpose.

Against that background, I want to turn now to the specific actions Ford Motor Company will take to carry out its responsibilities in the area of pollu-

tion control. To the extent possible, we are concerned with results *now* and in the near-term range up to 10 years from now.

Number One — The major obstacle to a quick and dramatic reduction in total automobile emissions is the fact that about 60 million older cars are in use that are not equipped with any kind of exhaust emission controls. Many of these cars will continue in use for years to come.

Our scientists tell me that, if every pre-1970 model car in the Los Angeles basin could be replaced immediately with a current model, hydrocarbon air pollution from automobile sources would fall below the level that prevailed in Los Angeles in 1940. Carbon monoxide emissions would fall below the 1950 level.

Because this is impossible, it is important to consider whether a lesser but still large reduction in total emissions could be achieved if emission controls could be developed for installation on older cars.

We are now conducting tests, on a limited scale, of a used-car air-pollution control kit based on the experience we have had with devices used on our new cars. Preliminary indications are that we could sell this kit at a price that might permit installation at a cost to the car owner as low as $50, and that it will reduce hydrocarbon and carbon monoxide emissions from pre-1968 Ford-built cars by as much as 50 percent.

We have discussed these developments with the Federal Government and have proposed a large-scale cooperative field test of the feasibility of this approach, conducted at our expense but utilizing one or more government automobile fleets. This field test will provide a good indication of the effectiveness and the cost of this approach, given the great variations which exist in the condition of used cars, the way they are driven and the skills of mechanics.

Even if field tests should confirm our preliminary findings, it is doubtful that many owners of older cars would voluntarily pay to have emission controls installed. The primary purpose of this program is to develop sound information that can be used by legislatures and government agencies in deciding whether or not to require installation of emission controls in older cars.

Number Two — Engine tuning and maintenance play a very important role in emission control. We will therefore make available to independent garages, as well as to our own dealers, a newly developed and greatly improved instrumentation system which measures hydrocarbon and carbon monoxide emissions during steady-speed engine operation in a garage environment. This instrument, developed by our Ford Service Research Center in cooperation with Honeywell, is already being delivered to some Ford dealers.

Ford Motor Company has for years advocated mandatory vehicle inspection by all states, principally for safety reasons. Now, with increasing emphasis on reducing vehicle emissions, we believe it even more essential that periodic engine checks and any necessary engine tuneups be required of all vehicles. Our new instrumentation system does not provide refined measurement of vehicle emissions under all operating conditions, but it does provide a quick, simple and inexpensive way of detecting the cars that are the worst offenders. It also helps a mechanic to determine which engine adjustments are needed and indicates whether his adjustments are adding to or cutting back exhaust emissions.

Number Three — The IIEC program will be completed a year from now, in December, 1970. During 1971 we will draw upon the results of this program and of our other research to develop experimental vehicles containing new emission control equipment that will be well ahead of current government requirements.

Before the end of 1971, we will offer to sell a number of these vehicles to large private fleet operators. This will give us an earlier field evaluation of this equipment and will thereby provide a realistic demonstration of customer service requirements and of whatever penalties may be expected in the way of initial cost, performance, reliability, serviceability, durability and cost of maintenance.

Number Four — We will make the same offer to federal, state and city fleet operators, who would then have an opportunity to devise their own testing and maintenance procedures for these cars. We will also offer to lend a limited number of experimental low-emission cars to pollution control authorities in both California and Washington, D.C., for their cooperative evaluation.

As you may know, bills have recently been introduced in both houses of Congress that would require the General Services Administration to purchase for government use cars which surpass current emission standards by a specified margin, even though a cost penalty will be involved. Without commenting on the details of the bills, we think that this is an excellent concept.

Such legislation would not, of course, provide an answer to all the technical problems that still need to be solved. If properly drawn, however, it could create a market which does not now exist. It would thereby strengthen competitive incentives and provide a realistic opportunity to test the economic and technical feasibility of incremental progress in reducing vehicle emissions. This, in turn, will provide a better basis for orderly tightening of the standards governing vehicles sold to the general public. We believe this proposal will be passed and I can promise you that Ford Motor Company will be competing vigorously in the new market it will create.

Number Five — To insure that the cars and trucks we produce do in fact have a low level of emissions, we will continue to strengthen our quality control procedures at every plant.

This month we are starting an experimental procedure at our Wayne Assembly Plant to find a feasible way to screen 100 percent of our vehicle production for abnormal emission levels, and thus minimize the problem at the source. If this procedure proves effective, we will adopt it at other assembly plants. Three other plants covering all of our car lines have full emission test laboratories where vehicles are spot-checked every day. In addition, we have a thoroughly instrumented and pressure-controlled room at our carburetor plant where 100 per-

cent of our carburetors are "flowed" and checked to be certain they are within necessary emission control tolerances.

Number Six — The emission level from motor vehicles and the cost and effectiveness of emission controls are influenced not only by the design of vehicles but also by the fuel they use. Engines, control devices and fuels have to be designed as a single system if maximum results are to be achieved.

As I have mentioned, we are working closely with a number of oil companies and other auto companies to develop new ways of reducing emissions. IIEC research has been directed along two lines. One involves changes in fuel composition — mainly the elimination of lead additives — along with the use of new devices such as thermal reactors and catalytic converters. This approach appears to offer great potential.

The second approach recognizes that the petroleum industry would need several years to convert to non-leaded gasoline and would incur costs that might have to be reflected in higher gasoline prices. This approach, which seeks to develop a system that would

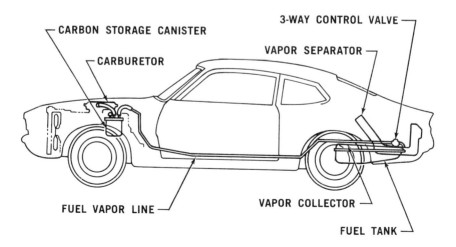

FORD FUEL SEAL SYSTEM

CARBON STORAGE CANISTER
3-WAY CONTROL VALVE
CARBURETOR
VAPOR SEPARATOR
FUEL VAPOR LINE
VAPOR COLLECTOR
FUEL TANK

work with leaded gasoline, has been less successful to date.

Within the next year, the IIEC program expects to have firm recommendations as to the best combination of engine design, control devices and fuel composition to meet future emission standards.

I should point out here that the potential cost of changes in gasoline is only one of the many trade offs that must be considered as we work toward the goal of cleaner air and water. Other trade offs involve such values as vehicle performance and durability, fuel economy and ease of maintenance and serviceability. We will make available to government authorities as much comparative information on these subjects as we can so that they in turn will be better able to establish standards that will best serve the public interest.

Number Seven — Although further refinement of internal combustion engines and fuels is clearly the most promising route in our search for a lower-emission vehicle, we will continue our efforts to develop other power sources.

We have a strong vested interest in the survival of the internal combustion engine, but we have a far stronger interest in the survival of our Company. It would be foolhardy for us to stand by and let others take the lead in efforts to make the internal combustion engine obsolete.

We have been working on possible alternatives to the reciprocating internal combustion engine for many years — on turbines since 1952, on electric power since 1956, on gasoline-electric hybrid concepts since 1960, on steam engines since 1953 and on still other approaches throughout the past decade.

Our work on low emission power sources must be governed, however, by sensible priorities. The effort devoted to any particular approach must bear a reasonable relationship to the chances for its success.

On the basis of our own research and thorough study of the available information on work done by others, we are giving top priority to the development of improved and cleaner versions of the internal combustion engine. This is the approach that we believe will yield the best results from our research and development investment in the near future.

We have assigned second place in our priority list to the gas turbine. We are now testing turbine engines in regular service in our own truck fleet and a Ford turbine has recently been installed in a Continental Trailways bus. Low emission turbine engines will certainly be in regular commercial use in over-the-road trucks and buses during the seventies. We are also moving ahead on the much more difficult problem of developing a turbine engine suitable for passenger car use.

Our work on other approaches is on a much smaller scale which we believe is commensurate with the present outlook for their success and potential usefulness. We are continuing our work on the sodium-sulphur battery, which we invented, and on electric car concepts that may have limited application for short-range, low-speed urban and suburban travel. We are studying the potential of various hybrid power sources. Even though steam appears at this time to be the least promising substitute for the internal combustion engine, we are also doing studies in this area. In addition, we are continuing our search for new types of low emission engines through outside firms working under contract to us.

We are as aware as anyone is of the huge stake that could be won by the company that invents a practical, emission-free substitute for the internal combustion engine. Unfortunate as it may be, however, raising the stake does not improve the odds.

Others may disagree with our reading of the odds, and they may prove to be right. No one can be certain about the chances for technical breakthroughs that could change the whole outlook.

That is why we are staying active in research on a wide variety of possible substitutes for the internal combustion engine. We must be ready and able to change our priorities and shift our emphasis the moment we see evidence that the odds are changing. Meanwhile, we will continue to put most of our money on the internal combustion engine and a substantial amount on the gas turbine.

Number Eight — We recognize an equally serious responsibility to prevent our manufacturing plants from polluting the atmosphere and we are already well along in a program to accomplish those things that can be done *now* to reduce or eliminate this form of air pollution. A major problem here, just as with automotive emissions, is that the technology is not yet equal to the demand.

The best solution, when possible, is to start from scratch by moving an operation from an old facility to a new facility incorporating the latest pollution-free processes and the best pollution control equipment available. This is what we are doing with our Dearborn Iron Foundry, which will be shut down permanently when our new Castings Plant at Flat Rock, Michigan, is completed in 1971. The new plant will be the cleanest in the business, not only because of its pollution control equipment, but because it will make use of a melting process that substantially reduces the amount of pollutants being generated.

In 1971 we will also complete installation of a second generation of air pollution control equipment at our Cleveland Foundry. Foundries have traditionally been serious offenders and we have made them priority targets in our air pollution control program.

Number Nine — We will move ahead just as vigorously to reduce and virtually eliminate water pollution from our plants. We are confident that we will meet the established water quality standards well before the end of 1971.

At our new Kentucky Truck Plant, we have cooperated with local government authorities in establishing the nucleus of a waste water treatment plant that will provide collection and treatment facilities not only for our own plant but for all other users in a wide geographical area. By looking beyond our own needs, we are helping to benefit entire communities which also must share in the struggle to clean up our waters. We intend to offer this same leadership in other communities where Ford plants are operated.

During the past 10 years, we have spent $66 million on facilities and equipment to reduce air and water pollution from our plants, and we are now planning to spend nearly $60 million more during the next two years.

Number Ten — And finally, in still another phase of our attack on environment pollution, we will search for cleaner methods of disposing of non-salvageable solid and liquid wastes from our manufacturing operations.

At our Rouge Plant, we have leased a parcel of property to an outside contractor who will process a major portion of our waste material. Instead of burning those wastes, the contractor will extract reusable materials, then reduce the remainder to compact bundles and move the bundles to an appropriate landfill location. Because such locations are getting scarce, burning of some waste products may be preferable to landfill disposal in the long run. Therefore, we will work with incinerator manufacturers to develop high-temperature devices that do not give off objectionable particulate matter or gases. The small volume of inert materials resulting from this incineration will require very little space in landfill locations.

I hope I have conveyed to you both the magnitude of our anti-pollution planning and the deep sense of commitment with which we have approached the task. Ford Motor Company is doing all in its power to help achieve the goal of cleaner air and cleaner water.

PULP AND PAPER IS CONCERNED ABOUT WATER POLLUTION

Robert M. Schmon

Robert M. Schmon is the president of the Ontario Paper Company and its associated companies.

My company is a subsidiary of the Tribune Company, a holding company which publishes the Chicago Tribune, Chicago Today, the New York Daily News, and five newspapers in Florida, notably the Fort Lauderdale News and the Orlando Sentinel. The Canadian operations, with which I am concerned, include The Ontario Paper Company Limited which operates a newsprint mill and by-products plants at Thorold, Ontario and its subsidiary, Quebec North Shore Paper Company which operates a larger newsprint mill at Baie Comeau, Quebec. Our combined annual capacity is 550,000 tons of newsprint, increasing next year to 750,000 tons when an expansion at the Baie Comeau mill is completed.

Like all pulp and paper mills, we require large quantities of water. Our two mills combined use close to 50 mil-

lion gallons a day, about the same as a city of 300,000 people. We have two kinds of waste: suspended solids such as minute fibres and bark particles; and dissolved solids such as wood sugars, lignins, and cellulose organics. These wastes may adversely affect fish life and may present aesthetic problems but do not have the human health hazards of municipal waste.

The specific pollution problems in our two mills are poles apart. At Thorold we are in a highly industrialized and urbanized area. Our problem is compounded because our effluent flows through two communities with a total population of 115,000 on its way to a fresh water basin, Lake Ontario. At our Baie Comeau plant in the Province of Quebec we are in a remote area on salt water where tides run as high as 16 to 17 feet. This is another complexity of our industry. One mill may be located in a major metropolitan area, another is far off, still

Reprinted by permission of the author, Robert M. Schmon.

72

others are in medium size communities in relatively well developed areas. So there is no panacea for water pollution. Solutions must be tailor-made for each mill. This means money, lots of it. It also means time to develop and put into effect the right treatment at the right place. In spite of many significant accomplishments there is still a long way to go and a lot to learn.

In Canada, it seems to me that until the 1930's the priority with industrial developers and government leaders on federal, provincial, and municipal levels was to encourage economic development and expansion without regard to the cumulative impact of pollution. No one, it seemed, considered that the vast natural wealth of our inland water system would be endangered by human interference. Perhaps there was a sense of false security because Canada has 9% of the total flow of all rivers in the world and only 1% of the population. The simple fact is that these vast water resources *are* endangered and something must be — and is being — done about it.

I want to emphasize strongly that *all* society has contributed to water pollution. *All* society has a responsibility to overcome it. No one in industry, government, or the public can afford to just point the finger at the other fellow. It is *everybody's* business.

The pulp and paper industry in Canada recognizes its responsibility and the need for a sustained program to reduce or eliminate harmful effects of its effluents on the environment. Detailed data compiled by co-operative task forces show that in the period 1960 through 1966, mills accounting for 75% of total Canadian production installed recovery facilities costing more than $64 million, appreciably reducing the pollution load. (This is about 5% of the total capital expenditure during that period.) I am not try-ing to make a case here that the industry has done everything it should, but what I am trying to say is that it has a done a great deal more than it is given credit for.

In our own company we can date pollution abatement activities back to 1935 when we established our research department and stipulated that one of its prime objectives was to reduce pollution and waste by fostering development of profitable new products from our effluent. Since then we have spent more than $4 million in research and development on by-products alone. Our research expenditures have now accelerated and we are spending about 50% of the total research budget in the by-product and pollution abatement areas. We have spent or are committed to spend more than $16 million capital in waste utilization and removal. These are considerable sums to a Canadian company like ours with annual sales of a little over $100 million.

In 1943 we built the first commercially successful plant in North America producing ethyl alcohol from spent sulphite liquor. The process was an adaptation of previous European practices. This plant, still in operation, removes some 25 tons a day of sugars from our effluent. In 1952 we started our own patented process to make vanillin, a synthetic vanilla, which removes 25 tons of other organics. These two by-product operations which constitute 8% of our gross sales, produce revenue. However, not everyone can make alcohol or vanillin. The markets are limited, but it is the route we chose. Perhaps we were fortunate. The great Canadian humorist, Stephen Leacock, once remarked that he believed in luck but found that the harder he worked the luckier he got.

But if I or anyone in our management today get too heady with these successes we remind ourselves that a few years ago we invested in an oxalic acid plant that ran into technical and market difficulties and we had to close it down this spring. Not everything works in this struggle. In addition, our vanillin plant, while reducing the biological oxygen demand of our waste, creates an aesthetic problem due to colour and foam. So improving your effluent may sometimes be like transforming your wife into a Raquel Welch with some miracle drug only to find out the drug has an unfortunate side effect — she can't stand the sight of you anymore.

So be it for yesterday. Now we must move faster. The condition of our environment and the temper of our times impatiently demand action. Regulatory bodies, encouraged by public opinion, are pressing for water quality standards that will require considerable investment and effort on industry's part. Nonetheless the job must be done.

The exact cost faced by our industry is difficult to establish, in part through lack of uniformity in legislation across Canada and in part through the lack of proven technology in some aspects of pollution abatement. However, it is estimated that stream pollution abatement in Canada's paper industry could require more than $250 million in capital funds, with annual operating charges of some $40 million. This does not include prior treatments such as evaporation and burning which could add to these already high costs. Such expenditures could significantly weaken the Canadian industry's competitive position in world markets. Most of these expenditures will be for one purpose only — to maintain and improve the environment. They will not increase productivity and, in most cases, there will be no financial return.

Our own company has just announced at the Thorold mill a $5 million program over two years which we hope will get us to the point of removing at least 85% of both dissolved and suspended solids. We hope to accomplish this through external treatment for suspended solids and an evaporation and burning process for dissolved solids. We are researching a process to recover reusable chemicals to reduce operating costs of this program to a break-even point. To approach this, at least an additional $3 million will be involved, and we will be lucky to achieve this objective. The risk is increased operating costs anywhere up to $5.00 per ton.

Any further improvement from this point, will very sharply increase our costs. To use the words of one of our experts — "the leaner the effluent, the fatter the bill". So we are faced with the delicate task of meeting exacting current and future standards in a time of relentlessly rising costs while still keeping our business on a sound economic basis not only for our shareholders, but for our customers, employees, suppliers, and the communities in which we live.

I do not regard this as all bad news. The pressures being exerted on us will force us to improve our technology, continuing the search for new by-products, recoverable chemicals, and tighter in-plant measures. But I suggest the industry must look beyond that to major breakthroughs in pulping and paper-making techniques that will minimize pollution by reducing effluents, and by finding profitable uses for the effluents that are produced.

However, that may be papermaking in the 21st century. It does not negate the fact that we are facing the problem now, recognizing that some of the large investment we have in plant and equipment may have to be scrapped or changed radically.

The pulp and paper industry occupies a position of considerable importance in Canada's economy. It accounts for 1/7 of Canada's total exports and is one of the country's leading employers. Its growth and position as a major provider of employment and foreign exchange would be impaired if it must face alone the tremendous cost burden of pollution abatement. We have been advised by federal and provincial government representatives that anti-pollution measures should be included as part of production costs, and I presume they mean passed on to the customer. Looking at it realistically, we are not going to be able to pass on all these costs. It is for this reason that I, along with my colleagues in the industry, seek assistance from the three levels of government in Canada.

There are several ways in which we think the governments could legitimately and justifiably provide incentives. I refer specifically to such items as sales taxes on equipment used in pollution abatement. Why should we pay these? Why should municipalities increase our property and building evaluations when we are spending money for public benefit? We could be greatly assisted if the federal government would improve recovery of expenditure through more advantageous depreciation rates and make funds available at low interest rates to industries undertaking approved abatement programs.

Lastly, I would caution against pushing industry into unnecessary expenditures in the understandable haste to control pollution. I have already indicated the differences between our own problems in our two locations. In one — as with other mills in remote areas — we can install satisfactory

pollution controls at substantially less cost. What I am suggesting is that the different situations facing each plant should be recognized and that blanket and inflexible directives and regulations should not be imposed. It would be illogical to insist on treatment just for treatment's sake.

I am particularly aware of this because at the moment the regulatory situation in Canada is under review. Each province has its own regulatory body but the federal government is presenting to the current session of Parliament a new Canada Water Act designed to give common policy across the country. The Act advocates, among other things, regional boards with representatives from government and industry. I think this is a useful step, not only to provide a much-needed exchange of technical and research data, but to permit examination of all sides of the problem, to establish realistic and attainable timetables, and to develop co-operative information programs to acquaint the public with what is being done.

I emphasize that this last point is one of the chief problems. It is unfortunate that the good deeds of industry do not get equal publicity with the bad. A company can announce a major pollution control undertaking and the story is tucked away on a back page. On the other hand if a company is notified to improve its program or is fined for not doing enough, that news lands on page one and the adverse reaction of the public is reflected on industry generally. For the man in the street, it is often difficult to realize that something has been done and is being done because there is a sizeable time lag not only through the research stage but in the actual implementation. In the program we announced last month at Thorold, it will be two years before the public will see any obvious effect. I am sure that in the next two years we are going to receive a lot of adverse comment despite our program and the announcements we have made about it.

So money and technology are not enough. There must also be understanding. Without it we cannot marshall the full force of our society to control water pollution. That is the essential point I want to make. The public is concerned. The government is concerned. I can assure you that my company and the Canadian pulp and paper industry are concerned. Let us now try to understand each other's problems and desires so that we may move together more effectively toward environmental improvements that will provide conditions for healthful and pleasant living which all of us have every right to expect and enjoy.

GARDEN CITY PAPER FINED FOR POLLUTION

Larry Sicinski

Garden City Paper Mills Co. Ltd., a division of Canadian International Paper Co., was found guilty of polluting the province's waterways and fined $700 in provincial court here yesterday.

After hearing evidence from the Ontario Water Resources Commission and Garden City representatives, Judge Marc Girard rejected a not guilty plea by the company and gave it 30 days to pay the fine.

During the five-hour trial, OWRC chemical engineer John D. Luyt, of the industrial wastes division, told the court that samples of the Turner Cres. mill effluent taken Jan. 15 revealed discharges, with acidic contents above the acceptable level, had been made into a watercourse flowing into the Old Welland Canal and, ultimately, into Twelve Mile Creek and Lake Ontario.

OWRC tests recorded a PH reading of 2.2 on the day in question, well in excess of the 5.5 minimum standard of acidity content set by the commission.

Indicating a PH reading of 2.2 had a number of detrimental effects, Mr. Luyt said an acid content such as that could corrode concrete and would only support "species of fungus."

"A PH content as low as 2.2 will support no aquatic life," he added.

J. L. G. Keogh, counsel representing Garden City, denied the polluting charge, claiming that the company had installed neutralizing equipment meeting the requirements laid down by the

Reprinted with permission of *St. Catharines Standard,* June 6, 1970.

OWRC, but the filtration system had broken down Jan. 13 and was inoperable on the day in question through no fault of the company.

He told the court that shutting down the parchment machine, which would have prevented dumping the pollutants in the watercourse until the neutralizing equipment was repaired and reinstalled, would have had "serious effects."

Ten men would have been out of work for three days and one shift, costing them about $750 in wages, and the production schedule of the mill would not have been met.

The defence did not deny the certificate of analysis produced by the OWRC of the Jan. 15 sampling. In fact, it was revealed — through testimony of Peter Parent, plant general superintendent — that acidity content in PH tests conducted by the company from May, 1969, to Jan., 1970, had shown readings ranging from 2.2 to 4.7 even when the neutralizing equipment was in operation.

However, Mr. Parent indicated that the acidic content of the effluent before neutralizing facilities were initially installed was worse. He felt that the acidic content in the effluent had improved and, thus, was acceptable.

"Acceptable by you, sir?" Judge Girard questioned.

"Yes," replied Mr. Parent, who earlier had admitted having no professional chemical training and had indicated he was unaware of OWRC acidity content minimum standards.

Crown Attorney Lloyd Goodwin, in summarizing, submitted that the defendant company had set no objectives in reducing their pollution and was only seeking a simple reduction in acidity to "attempt to comply with written words" in their certificate of approvals granted earlier by the OWRC.

He implied that Garden City and "other industries" had only provided an "imagined" or "cynical" compliance with the regulations.

Mr. Goodwin called for the maximum penalty to make it clear that this court and other courts treat this act seriously.

"The enforcement must become more rigorous," he added.

"It's just like someone dumping his garbage on the street and saying to the rest of society, 'Here, you look after it.'"

In finding the company guilty, Judge Girard pointed out that the fact that water quality had been impaired on Jan. 15 was "not particularly disputed."

Garden City is the first area paper mill to be convicted under Section 27 (1) of the OWRC Act which deals with discharge of materials capable of impairing the quality of water. Maximum penalty under the act is $1,000.

Part 4

The depth of public awareness of pollution problems is apparently not very great. Some observers fear that environmental concerns have become a fad: that young people looking for a cause to take up have adopted ecology in the same manner that they might adopt a new hair style, or a new pop music idol. The bandwagon may provide the quantity of bodies who will show concern — will it provide the quality of commitment to bring about radical changes? Those who have been in the vanguard of the movement are hopeful that the seriousness of the issue will provide its own impetus for reform.

ENVIRONMENT: WHILE THERE IS STILL TIME

The sensation in Vancouver was of a strange, if exhilarating, unreality. For a few days earlier this month, it seemed as if time had suddenly slipped into reverse, transporting the people of British Columbia's lower mainland back to the clear, sun-dappled days of childhood. The smoggy haze that usually hovers around Vancouver had magically disappeared. Across the grey-blue waters of the Georgia strait, Vancouver Island's whitecapped mountains could be seen for the first time in years. Even the scummy reaches of False Creek, a murky industrial inlet in the middle of the city, sparkled in the sun. So complete was the metamorphosis that the city seemed almost a stranger to itself. "It is something we have not experienced within memory," wrote a Vancouver *Sun* columnist. "This is Valhalla, the Utopia the pollution vigilantes are striving toward."

In this instance, Utopia lasted only briefly, the unusual result of a combination of perfect weather and labor trouble. What Premier W. A. C. Bennett likes to call the Good Life became appreciably better when overlapping strikes shut down pulp mills, stopped tugboats, silenced sawmills. For many British Columbians, the ensuing freedom from some of the more undesirable sights and smells of industry understandably came at too high a price. But in a curious, upside-down kind of way, Vancouver's respite underscored an issue that is occupying an increasing number of Canadians. The issue is this: at what stage do the trappings of technological society turn into an insupportable version of Mark Twain's "all the modern inconveniences"? And how far can the despoliation of the environment be justified in the name of the gross national product?

Until recently, it was considered rank heresy to question the theology of growth (and, to a large extent in B.C., it still is). Even less was it thought that Canada could ever run out of room for more and more people industriously practising the Puritan ethic of production while pursuing the more modern virtue of consumption. For one thing, there was the comfortable illusion that on the spaceship earth, Canadians would always travel first class, provisioned with an inexhaustible store of resources. Canada, after all, is endowed with 25 percent of the earth's fresh water, 17 percent of its softwood trees, 6 percent of its land surface — and just ½ of 1 percent of its population.

Cancerous growth

To those who have surveyed Canada's vastness, the land appears to be blessed with infinite physical resilience. Yet that illusion, too, is fast disappearing. Airline pilots on polar routes now report a grey-orange tinge in layers of air over the empty fastness of the Arctic. They say it is smog. Biologists have discovered chlorinated hydrocarbons in the fat of Arctic polar bears, telltale evidence of the wind-borne persistence of DDT. In place of the traditional image of a land of unlimited largesse, there is a quite different way of looking at Canada. It is as an industrialized nation still with time to call a halt to the cluttering of the landscape, with an excellent opportunity to overcome the crowding threats to its natural heritage. "Canada is lucky. We have a chance to read the breakdown signals and do something about them," says University of British Columbia Ecologist Crawford S. Holling. Like Dr. Holling, environmentalists who preach the new crusade believe it can be won only with a basic shift in social values. Dr. Arthur Cordell, an economic adviser to Ottawa's Science Council, puts the point vividly: "Growth for growth's sake is the ideology of the cancer cell."

On his recent Australian tour, Pierre Trudeau suggested that "perhaps the responsibility for acting decisively should fall with the greatest force upon countries such as ours, which are gifted with almost limitless space. We have, after all, the most to gain." The P.M. saw the options in Thoreauvian terms: "Life is not enriched if the cost of new automobiles and miracle synthetic products is fouled atmosphere and polluted rivers. Those great spaces which so many regard with indifference will prove, I suggest, to be our salvation. They are our escape from the pressures of civilization, the balance wheel of our personal machinery," He went on: "The issue is not simply one of litterbugs, or of offensive smells, as some industrialists would have us believe. The issue is one of life itself."

Usually the problem is not posed in such cosmic terms. Instead the evidence of environmental destruction appears piecemeal, a daily chronicle of human shortsightedness. Last week brought its full share of horrors. In Alberta, the provincial government was caught with its contingency plans down when an oil pipeline sprang a leak, spilling 574,500 gals. of synthetic crude in the Athabasca River area; much of the oozy goo spread 177 miles downstream to Lake Athabasca. In Quebec, a team from Asbestos Corporation Ltd. was trying to figure out just how much of the 420,000 gals. of diesel and aviation fuel that had leaked from storage tanks in Hudson Strait earlier this month had seeped into the sea.

With high summer approaching, there were more reminders than ever that people simply cannot enjoy the countryside as much anymore. In recent years, innumerable beaches have been posted with NO SWIMMING signs. This year, in Ontario, they are accompanied by new warning signs on recreational lakes. "Fish for fun," the signs admonish. "Fish from these waters should not be eaten because of mercury contamination." By that token, Hudson Bay should be posted. Last week, Northwest Territories' Commissioner Stuart Hodgson announced that thousands of cans of beluga whale meat would have to be destroyed because they contained twice the allowable amount of mercury. The whales had apparently ingested the mercury from the outflow of the industrially contaminated South Saskatchewan River.

A willingness to pay

So frequent have these micro-disasters become that there is hardly a Canadian who is not in one way or another sensitive to the dangers facing his environment. In a recent Gallup poll, 69 percent of the sample rated Canada's pollution problems as very serious. Only 3 percent did not feel in any way threatened. Another poll carried out by an antipollution group in New Westminster, B.C., suggested that people are prepared to pay for solutions; a full 71 percent of the respondents said they would be willing to pay higher taxes to control pollution. But these figures do not do justice to the emotions that the word environment can arouse. In the past two or three years, it has become a catchword that has swept the country with the speed and force of an idea whose time has come. In some instances, its implications are so poorly defined that there is a danger that the word may die of popularity before it is fully understood. Even so, the impact of the new concern is so great that a standard excuse for past mistakes is that they were committed "before people cared."

That care manifests itself in many ways. Its most obvious form is in the dozens of acronymic environmental groups that are burgeoning across Canada, including GASP (Group Action to Stop Pollution), STOP (Save Tomorrow — Outlaw Pollution) and SPEC (Society for Pollution and Environmental Control). There are at least 50 of these across the country now, and their crusades encompass virtually every environmental problem from the population explosion through phosphates and superhighways to the preservation of the tailed toad.

Overexposure

So quickly have the citizens' action groups proliferated that they run some risks. One is that they can be too concerned with quick, *ad hoc* solutions whose implications are not always clear. Dr. Fred Knelman, who heads a new department of science and human values at Montreal's Sir George Williams University, is now trying to coordinate the various groups across the country into a national environmental council. "Many groups work in a self-defeating way since not enough people understand the problem," he says. "Many have too simplistic a view." A second danger is overexposure. Says Zoologist Donald Chant, the mentor of Toronto's Pollution Probe: "The public is at last aware of the dangers of pollution. What I am afraid of now is that they will become so appalled by reading one story after another that, in self-protection, they will turn themselves off."

The evangelists have certainly inculcated awareness. In steel-making Hamilton, and in Montreal and Toronto, what used to be called "heat haze" is now known by its proper name — air pollution. Along with temperature and humidity readings, the newspapers now run daily counts that help to explain why it is difficult, if not downright hazardous, to breathe downtown. Ontario started the trend last March when it instituted Toronto's Air Pollution Index, a scale based on the amount of sulphur dioxide and particulates in the atmosphere. When the index reaches 32, the government can ask polluters to close down; at 50, the request becomes a demand. So far, the scale has reached 32 on six occasions, and in each instance polluters have complied with the government. The major polluter in the cities is the automobile, and here again Ontario has taken the lead by legislating against excessive auto exhaust. For its part, Ottawa is "studying" the question of auto exhaust. One thing that should make its task easier was the setting up last April of an air pollution control division in the federal health department, with 70 air sampling stations in 14 cities.

A new Toronto firm called Pollution City Devices Ltd. has been pleasantly surprised by the concern for the noxious city air. It has just put on the market a gadget called Emisco, which makes the combustion in auto engines more efficient during acceleration, deceleration and idling, and thus cuts down on exhaust. The cost is $24.95 installed. The odd point about Emisco is that it was introduced eight years ago, before people cared about pollution, as an economy device called Gas-O-Miser, and bombed. Now, in just three weeks, the firm has already installed 400 for delivery fleets. Reported one customer: "The results were staggering. The carbon monoxide emission dropped from 8 percent to 1 percent.

The ubiquitous reminders of the abuse of Canada's air, land and water are hardly surprising in view of the extraordinary amount of detritus that even a supposedly underpopulated country produces. The average Canadian gets through 5 lbs. of refuse a day, a figure that is rising about 7 percent every year. Former Tory Party President Dalton Camp regularly summers in a pastoral corner of his native New Brunswick, but even there, he complains that "I get the general feeling that I am slowly being surrounded by garbage, a closing circle of non-returnable bottles." His point is buttressed by

an interesting experiment carried out by Nova Scotia high school students. Working under the provinces highways department, the youngsters took an inventory of the roadside litter along selected mile-long stretches of road. In a single mile, they picked up 4,908 items, including more than 1,000 candy wrappers, 350 cigarette packages, 673 beer, pop and liquor bottles, 388 cans, 20 old tires, 26 shoes, 17 fruit and vegetable discards, 30 pieces of clothing and nine dead animals, including a horse.

The littered landscape is partly the result of consumer demand that everything should be disposable these days, and industry's response with containers that are not biodegradable. This year, for example, the country will get through 5 billion cans and 2 billion bottles, many of them non-returnable —or as the advertising says, "one-way" containers. Ontario and several other provinces are waiting to see how a new British Columbia law will work out which hopes to ease the problem by requiring the manufacturers to charge a two-cent deposit on every beer and soft drink bottle and can. (Unfortunately, the B.C. legislation exempts the 87 million cans made in the province— 96 percent of all can sales.) Ominously, there seems to be no stop to the cult of disposability. The International Paper Co. is now talking about a complete throwaway environment for babies. One Montreal importer is even trying to sell paper panties. "You wear them and then just throw them away," say the ads. "Pick up a six-pack today."

Of all the environmental deprivations Canadians have imposed on themselves, water pollution is the most dismaying. The history of the lovely St. John River Valley presents the classic case. Once one of the continent's great salmon rivers, the St. John periodically goes dead in some

stretches. From the U.S. border to a few miles above Fredericton, only 50,000 people live alongside the river. Yet the industrial waste poured into the St. John in that stretch is equivalent to the raw sewage of 3.3 million people. The major culprit is Fraser Companies Limited, whose pulp mills inject the equivalent waste of 2.4 million people into the river. So polluted has the St. John become that a 1½-year-old, $3.7 million fish hatchery below the Mactaquac Dam has turned into a macabre joke. Instead of helping produce new salmon, the river water was killing them, forcing federal fisheries experts to have the salmon incubated elsewhere in the Maritimes. Still, a belated cleanup is under way. This month a treatment plant for Fredericton is nearing completion. The only snag is that a new pulp mill upstream, complete with antipollution equipment, will add to the river slightly more waste than Fredericton will treat.

In an attempt to stimulate the St. John's tourist appeal, Premier Louis Robichaud is scheduled this week to open what he terms a "recreational masterpiece": a 60-mi.-long artificial lake behind the Mactaquac Dam. "At first sight one would take it for a freshwater paradise, a mecca for people in boats, for people swimming, for people fishing," wrote Novelist David (*Geordie*) Walker. "The regrettable fact, however, is that our lovely riverlake is dirty, smelly and virtually fishless. If you visit the most famous salmon pool of all, at Hartland, you will no longer see a line of fishermen casting over their own New Brunswick water. You will not see a single fisherman." Robichaud is working on that, too. The province has already ordered all industries throughout the province to install primary treatment plants by the start of 1972. If Fraser complies, says Federal Fish Biologist Paul Rug-

gles, that "will probably put the St. John back in business."

The trouble is that Canada is starting its water cleanup process at a very late stage. The most serious industrial problem is the pulp and paper industry which accounts for 60 percent of industrial water use. A large pulp mill uses up as much water as the City of Ottawa — and there are 180 of them across the country. But while it has been fashionable to criticize the beleaguered pulp and paper industry, it is far from being the only or even the principal villain. Since chemicals have replaced manures as fertilizers, agricultural runoff has done much to poison not only water, but fish and birds through the food-chain. But the greatest polluter is untreated sewage. Halifax, Quebec City, Hull and Victoria all still dump their raw sewage into water. Montreal pumps 500 million gals. of sewage into the St. Lawrence every day, of which only 8 percent receives any kind of treatment at all. Almost certainly, treatment of municipal sewage is going to be the most difficult water abuse to clean up. In Nova Scotia alone it has been estimated that it will cost $150 million to solve the problem. The main obstacle is the reluctance of the average ratepayer, who until recently has been unwilling to go along with the discovery of the animals in Walt Kelly's *Pogo* that "we have met the enemy and he is us."

A good share of the credit for alerting popular attention to the threatened environment belongs to the scientists of the federal Canadian Wildlife Service, who were once apt to be dismissed as nature nuts. Now they are heroes of the movement for their persistent warnings that there was more danger in the insecticides like DDT than at first met the eye. Tony Keith, head of the service's pesticides section, is the man who first put Biologist Norvald Fimreite on the track of mercury pollution in Canada's waters. "Wildlife," says Keith, "are useful and terribly expendable indicators of what's happening to our environment. Their plight brings up the whole question of what kind of landscape we want to live in." The Canadian Wildlife Service has compiled a list of 72 endangered species, and geographic populations in Canada. Among the vanishing breeds:

• The peregrine falcon was once described as "the embodiment of noble rapacity and lonely freedom." In Canada, the falcon is certainly lonely, though it is not exceptionally shy of man. In 1938, a female yearling nested in the gutters of Montreal's Sun Life building, eventually returning year after year and raising 22 young. Now no falcons remain in the East, and only two pairs have been reported east of Alberta. What is killing the falcon, along with the bald eagle, the osprey and Richardson's pigeon hawk, is the persistence of insecticides based on chlorinated hydrocarbon compounds, chief of which is DDT.

• In Newfoundland (but not the Arctic), the Arctic Hare has nearly been driven out by the competition for food from the varying hare and the moose, both introduced by man. Ironically, it appears to be recovering now because poor logging practices are creating the barren Arctic habitat on which the hare thrives. An ill omen.

• On lonely Sable Island, off the coast of Nova Scotia, the Ipswich Sparrow has so far survived an even crazier ecological merry-go-round. First, the sparrows' food was endangered by imported rabbits. Rats, which swam to the island from shipwrecks, reduced the rabbits but threatened the sparrows' nests. Cats were brought in to kill the rats, but multiplied out of control. Then men brought dogs, and started to shoot the cats. Four thousand of the sparrows survive, but they face at least one inexorable threat: the island is sinking into the sea at a rate of half an inch a century.

Doom and gloom

Of all Canada's citizen activists, perhaps the most effective is Pollution Probe's Donald Chant. The group was started last year to stop fluoride poisoning of cattle caused by the Electric Reduction Co. in Dunnville, Ont. It now has six full-time paid coordinators and a formidable list of victories, including successful campaigns against DDT and phosphates. Chant shows a sure sense of theater. P.P.'s exploits have included a mock inquest of poisoned ducks, and a telegenically staged funeral service for Toronto's polluted Don River. Chant is careful not to put all the blame on scapegoats. "Industry is catering to the desires of all of us," he says. "But industry is defensive, reluctant, uses specious arguments to defend its record: it will not take effective action unless forced into it by government."

British Columbia's Municipal Affairs Minister Dan Campbell recently inveighed against "professors in their ivory towers and teachers in their little cubicles who are spreading 'doom and gloom' about the extent of pollution in the country." Fortunately, the charge seems to be quite true. In high schools, environmental studies are becoming more and more in vogue, often functioning as the basis for hundreds of do-it-yourself projects. At the university level, the approach to environmental problems is becoming increasingly sophisticated, tending toward interdisciplinary teams studying specific themes.

One of the most fascinating programs is that of Ecologist Crawford Holling at U.B.C. Working with a 45-

man team and $1,000,000 Ford Foundation grant, Holling is tackling environmental imponderables with a computer. His first project, which took two years, was to set up a scientific model of B.C.'s Gulf Islands by feeding into the computer 60 years' worth of information about land uses and needs, ecology, market forces and speculation trends. The computer reached the depressing conclusion that 80 percent of all first-class recreational land on the beautiful islands will be developed by 1980, a finding that prompted the provincial government to impose a minimum 10-acre lot size for future subdivision. Holling's next experiment is a five-year survey of B.C.'s lower mainland water resources which he hopes will find a way "into the real world, via legislation, zoning variances, city and regional plans."

What such studies promise is a way to avoid the gross mistakes of such projects as the W. A. C. Bennett Dam. There is also obvious need for far more sensitive coordination of environmental policies within and between governments at all levels. Over the last year, there has been a flurry of environmental legislation in Ottawa and the provincial capitals. The Federal Government is regulating the use of phosphates in detergents, has outlawed the indiscriminate use of DDT and launched a whole new raft of anti-pollution bills. Its major move against water abuse is the Canada Water Act, now before the Senate, and aimed at creating joint governmental management water-quality agencies for every region, river or lake basin threatened by pollution. The bill's major weakness, apart from being inadequately funded, is that it could turn into a bureaucratic monster. Ottawa's second important initiative is the Arctic pollution bill, which bespeaks a real determination to preserve the delicate ecology of the North from the same kind of depredations that are taking place on Alaska's North Slope.

Health Minister John Munro has been talking about a clean air bill for more than a year, but that idea is still up in the air. Fisheries Minister Jack Davis' tough amendments to the Fisheries Act are now before Parliament. They would in effect give the minister the right to block construction of any industrial plant that might have a capacity for polluting fish — a wide mandate indeed. But more is needed. Says Chant: "There was a very adequate bill passed in 1843 which prohibited putting anything in the waters of Canada that is harmful to fish. It would have done the job very well if we had chosen to make it effective."

Davis may be just the man to push tougher enforcement. He has already succeeded in breaking the long bureaucratic tradition of tiptoeing through the messy area of industrial responsibility for water problems. His policy, which is rapidly becoming federal policy, runs the risk of being oversimplified, but is often fair enough: the polluter must pay. Says Davis: "If environmental considerations become the fundamental backdrop against which everything is assessed — if we look at what a plant is likely to do before it is built — we'll be all right."

New indicators

Despite the hazard of conflicting constitutional jurisdictions, what is really needed is a federal effort to lead and shape the growing consensus for quality in life before it fizzles or fragments. The process of refining social choices and presenting the alternatives has only barely begun, and since many desirable environmental controls would cost a great deal of money, the politicians are not exactly rushing to be the first to break the news. Says John

Gordon, a senior civil servant in the Department of Indian Affairs and Northern Development: "The realities of hard politics are that, inevitably, the measures necessary to save our environment are going to run against the grain of other expectations. We are going to have to question the size and speed of our cars, whether every damn thing in the world has to be encased in a plastic bag and whether private property rights extend to all the things we have been used to thinking they do."

To replace the gross national product as the first yardstick of progress, a whole new series of indicators could well be useful. In Australia, Pierre Trudeau even suggested that it would be preferable to arrive at a "net national product" to measure the quality of national life. It would subtract from the G.N.P. the cost of activities that are detrimental to the environment. In the same vein, Dr. O. M. Solandt, chairman of the Science Council, proposes that a more appropriate measurement for cities than new factories might be the ratio of their acreage of parks to acreage of parking lots. If such concepts are still tentative, and the goals hazy, the danger signs in Canada's present course cannot be overlooked. Unless there is a conscious effort toward new approaches, most Canadians may one day find themselves living in a drab, chaotic world that nature never evolved and man never really intended.

WILL POLLUTION WAR DIE?

Ken Lefolii

Ken Lefolii is a staff writer for the Toronto Daily Star.

The most cynical hoax of the '60s was the War on Poverty, which, as you remember, Poverty won. Already it seems likely that the most cynical hoax of the '70s will be the assault on pollution.

Like poverty a few years ago, pollution now has everybody against it, all the time. On the political charts of America, Richard Nixon makes pollution one-two with crime in the streets.

In Canada, Pierre Trudeau makes pollution one-two with inflation. In the media, pollution has the top of the charts all to itself, number one in the magazines, number one on television, number one in the papers.

For how long?

How long will it be, do you suppose, before pollution becomes a bore? Before it loses the power to sell papers? Before politicians find they can safely revert to issues more easily solved? Judging by the archives of the War on Poverty, pollution would seem to have something like nine months left at the top of the charts.

Then what? Perhaps a sentimental

Reprinted with permission *Toronto Daily Star*, February 21, 1970.

revival every few years. This week Lester Pearson made a moving appeal on a religious television program for Canadian aid to the poor of underdeveloped countries.

Coming from the author of Canada's short, ignominious war on the poverty of a large part of her own population, this was the kind of preachment that gives piety a bad name.

At the very least, it must have made many members of Mr. Pearson's audience uneasy about the outcome of his successor's assault on pollution, which depends on most of the same weapons that lost the war on poverty — much rhetoric, some new regulations that may or may not be enforced, some allocations of money that may or may not be spent to any effect.

Their unease is shared by five scientists and an educator, from various parts of Canada, who joined me in a Toronto television studio the other night to set out, if they could, some steps that might still be taken against pollution.

Trust science. Dr. John Anderson, director of the Fisheries Research Board, St. Andrew's N.B., and a marine biologist with a striking record for strong, independent intelligence, believes that our abuse of the environment has reached "a biological Hiroshima stage," but that the technical problems raised at this stage are so complex that the public at large can never know much more about them than that they exist.

Scientists, he says, will have to provide the solutions and the conscience that will get them applied.

In fact, he reports, scientists in Canada are now forming "an umbrella-type organization representing the entire scientific enterprise to act as an informed conscience for Canada."

Eloquent though Dr. Anderson is, his colleagues were unconvinced. The new organization "presupposes that all of our environmental problems can be solved by science, and that's not true," says Dr. Donald Chant, the University of Toronto zoologist who founded Pollution Probe. "I admire, I support it, but it's not enough."

Start a political party. Dal Brodhead, a young activist in the Ontario Department of Education, believes people who want to see real solutions actually applied will have to form a political party "which exists for the sole and simple purpose of confronting the pollution issue across the country."

If you're a government scientist, quit. Dr. Crawford Holling, the distinguished ecologist who works at the University of British Columbia, was until three years ago on the staff of the federal forestry department.

"I didn't feel at all constrained about making any statements or doing any work directed toward maximizing production of that particular crop. But any statements concerning a misuse of our forest because it compromised wildlife or recreation or it caused massive run-offs — about statements of this kind I felt very profoundly constrained. And this was not just a feeling, but a directive. We were not to enter into that kind of controversy.

"The maddening thing was that the tools were there to do the job, and yet couldn't because of the characteristics of the institution. Now I hasten to add that this wasn't because the civil service mandarins were evil. They were just locked into their own history."

Dr. Holling, it seems to me, makes very plain indeed with these remarks the main reason why we in Canada almost never deal with our most pressing problems until they have passed the point where their worst results might still be prevented, and reached the stage where we can only attempt salvage.

As he says, government scientists, the very experts with whom we have placed the public trust to diagnose our national problems and devise their solutions, are openly ordered or quietly pressured to keep their mouths shut.

Any reporter who has tried to crowbar even mildly controversial information out of a government agency in Canada can confirm Dr. Holling's remarks.

Almost 10 years ago, when I was working on a magazine article about St. Lawrence pollution, I asked the Ontario government for some reports on industrial contamination. The reports were confidential, the government scientists said, but that shouldn't worry anybody since the agencies involved were collaborating with industry to remove the contamination. Publicity would only make the corporations in question less willing to collaborate, they said.

A year ago, when I was working on a book on the same subject, I asked the Ontario Water Resources Commission, the agency that now controls water quality in Ontario for information of the same kind.

The commission gave the same answer. During the intervening years all hope that the complete degradation of the streams I was interested in might be prevented at tolerable cost has disappeared. Restoring the water for any sane human use has become a salvage operation at a cost that is certainly exorbitant and may be out of reach.

Pray or fight. "We're talking about survival," Dr. Anderson says. "The thing is, I don't want to be dead or my children to be dead because of pollution. What distresses me is there are so many people in this country running around shouting about pollution and there aren't nearly enough people doing anything about it."

There's always a chance, of course, that there is no good reason to be uneasy about the Assault on Pollution. For moments when you're almost convinced that this time the rhetoric is for real, here is a final test. Say over twice this slogan:

Remember the War on Poverty.

POLLUTION PROBE BRANCH FORMS HERE

Andy Neimers

Andy Neimers writes on pollution for the St. Catharines Standard.

It may not yet have a home to call its own, but a branch of Pollution Probe has been formally organized in the Niagara Peninsula. And it has the blessing of The Committee of a Thousand.

The pollution-fighting branch organization was born Saturday morning at the United Auto Workers hall. Acting as temporary chairman was Dale O'Dell, chairman of the UAW's citizenship committee.

Four sub-committees were also established: Liaison, finance, publicity and projects, which produced the most interest and drew 17 members for a start.

Outside of politics

Using a starter kit booklet from the Pollution Probe group at the University of Toronto, Mr. O'Dell outlined the suggested functions of each group. He also emphasized that if the group was going to call itself Pollution Probe it could not take on affiliation with any political party.

The three-hour meeting was immediately followed by a short meeting of the projects committee at which former Welland alderman John Trufal acted as temporary chairman.

Herb Bailey took on the job of co-ordinating projects committee work in the Fort Erie area while Donna Skeoch took the St. Catharines chair on a temporary basis.

Committee members agreed that drawing up a list of major polluters in specific areas was a primary task. The whole branch will be meeting again April 11; the projects committee has set a meeting for April 4.

Daily air readings

Mr. Trufal also indicated that the projects committee would be asking provincial authorities if instruments would be installed in the city which would provide daily air pollution readings such as those announced Saturday for Toronto and Hamilton.

The liaison committee, meanwhile, is looking for a permanent home for the organization. Some time this week Brock University will be approached about space. Brock will also be asked to contribute its laboratory facilities for analysis of pollution specimens.

One of the matters left hanging for future meetings was the decision as to whether the group needed an executive

Reprinted with permission of the *St. Catharines Standard,* March 23, 1970.

because the Toronto group operates without one. Mr. O'Dell received the approval of assembled members that for now the chairman of the projects committee would also assume automatic title of vice-chairman.

Getting the last action at the organizational meeting was the finance committee. Discussion by the members indicated that a chairman was not immediately necessary since there were no funds with which to deal.

Financial support offered

This should change in the near future. Mr. O'Dell indicated that the UAW could be looked to for support and Mr. Trufal claimed several interested groups had made offers of support once Pollution Probe was officially born.

Saturday's meeting also saw the late arrival of Norm Mitchinson, vice-president of the Niagara Falls-based Committee of a Thousand.

Asked to comment, Mr. Mitchinson admitted to friction between his group last week and the yet unborn Pollution Probe.

"We were quite hurt last week," he claimed referring to a radio interview which suggested the group was inactive.

Mr. Mitchinson admitted the wound was healed.

Everyone vulnerable

"Pollution Probe has done a remarkable job," he stated, referring to the Toronto group.

Mr. Mitchinson warned Pollution Probe organizers to beware of being compromised. Everyone is vulnerable, he said, and through experience the Committee of a Thousand had found pressure could be applied to its members.

In conclusion, he offered the co-operation of the Niagara Falls organization and best wishes of success. The best wishes were tempered with the statement:

"I don't want you (the new group) to make a big splash and then peter out. It leaves a hell of a lot of skeletons in the closet that we have to clean up."

EARTH DAY

Senator Nelson

Senator Nelson is one of the leading advocates for pollution control in the U.S. Senate. He was a prime mover in the Earth Day program which did much to bring the issue to public attention.

Mr. Nelson. Mr. President, Earth Day was a tremendous nationwide success, bringing a far greater participation than I anticipated when I suggested the idea last September. Some 2,000 colleges, 10,000 high schools and grade schools and several thousand communities were involved.

For the past several weeks, along with many of my colleagues in Congress and along with many scientists, young people and environmentalists of all ages, I have participated in the events associated with Earth Day. It has been one of the most heartening of experiences to see such broad agreement wide participation and dramatically increased public understanding and concern about this challenge to America. It makes me believe for the first time that we can wage a successful war on our environmental problems.

It was clear too from Earth Day that the environmental concern is much broader than some people seem to understand. Far more than just a concern with wild rivers, the issue is one of the livability of the ghettos and the Appalachias, which are the worst environments in this country.

The question now on everybody's mind is — What next? What does Earth Day mean for the future? Where will it lead?

In my view, Earth Day's greatest meaning will be if it is seen as a beginning, not as a climax. The next step is the formation of environmental action groups in every community and campus in this country.

These groups must organize just as soon as possible to set specific goals to turn back the assault on our environment. The challenge will never be met from Washington alone, although the job now before Congress is to pass major, urgently needed legislation and to appropriate urgently needed funds on a scale as great as our spending for Vietnam or for new weapons systems.

The changes in attitudes, in priorities, and in the effectiveness of all our institutions, and the new emphasis on quality as well as quantity, will be effected only by a genuine, persistent grassroots effort. Community groups must build on the new public awareness of our grave environmental programs, testify at hearings and meetings from the city council to Congress, file court suits if necessary to bring action.

In this society, there is no substitute for an elightened citizen effort to meet the complex challenges of our age. This is as true today as it was two centuries ago.

Already, many groups have formed or are forming across the country

Reprinted from the *Congressional Record*, April 30, 1970.

which are providing a valuable foundation for a nationwide effort to improve our environment. In its recent and excellent special issue keyed to Earth Day, Look magazine listed a number of these national and regional organizations. These groups are to be commended for their efforts in the attack on the environmental deterioration that is one of the worst problems confronting us the world over, and I ask unanimous consent that their names be included in the Record at the end of these remarks.

The Presiding Officer. Without objection, it is so ordered.

Mr. Nelson. Mr. President, also special commendations are in order for the young people in the National Earth Day office in Washington and for everyone across the country who worked so hard to make Earth Day a success, and also for the excellent and thorough coverage of the programs and the environmental problems by the news media.

In the environmental fight, there is no question we have the resources and the technology to do the job. The only question is whether we have the will. Earth Day was a significant beginning.

Exhibit 1

WHAT DO YOU DO? HERE'S WHAT: JOIN THE FIGHT — "IF YOU'RE NOT PART OF THE SOLUTION, YOU'RE PART OF THE POLLUTION"

You can't escape it. No matter where you are, the crud is hitting you now. And it won't stop unless each of us makes a commitment to stop the environmental destruction going on all around us.

Every day, more Americans are taking action. The environmental movements is building fast from the grass roots. Thousands of citizen action groups have sprouted. In California alone, there are over 200 environmental community groups.

Americans of diverse occupations, backgrounds and beliefs are pooling their talents and energies. They have won battles in San Francisco Bay and Florida's Everglades. But there are many other fights, and *they need you*. To turn your alarm about the rape of the environment into action, pick up the telephone now. Call an environmental group to find out what you can do. Start by participating in nearby Earth Day activities.

Part 5

How much will it cost to clean up the mess? Who will pay? Where will the money go? What changes must we expect in our living habits? Will we be able to retain our freedom to do as we wish with what is ours? Can we afford pollution controls? Can we afford not to have pollution controls?

THE COST OF CLEANLINESS

Prime Minister Pierre Elliott Trudeau can speak plainly. The way to combat pollution, he said during one of his stops in the West, can only be through tough and costly methods. He suggested that criminal charges be brought against individuals and organizations that pollute natural resources. He warned that the cost of cleaning, and keeping clean, rivers and lakes and air and land will be great. He added, in his forthright fashion, we would have to pay up or shut up. And late last month his government announced the introduction of a new water act during the next Parliament, aimed at preventing the continuance of pollution.

His words were a jolt for those who have the murky ideas that "someone ought to do something". The "someone" is ourselves. And it is now apparent that we will have to pay dearly; for cleanliness, unlike Godliness, is expensive.

The slinking encroachment of pollution has been increasingly felt in the Atlantic Provinces. Placentia Bay, Newfoundland; Petitcodiac Lake near Moncton; and the St. John River valley are just three of a number of areas which have been in the news recently. The St. John has long been regarded as one of the best salmon rivers in the world, but now the cumulative effects of past pollution combined with biological and topographical changes caused by the construction of the Mactaquac Dam have seriously affected the salmon run. Remedies are being sought by the New Brunswick Water Authority, and biologists of the federal and provincial departments of fisheries.

Some idea of the costs involved in combating pollution can be gained from the St. John case. The response — stirred up through the urgings of the provincial government and a rising public opinion — has been good; both industries and communities are taking action to prevent further harmful wastes entering the river. The cost, though, has been high.

The Fraser Companies in Edmundston have already spent over $1-million in setting up anti-pollution procedures. Its mill will shortly switch from the sulphite to the kraft technique — which provides a means of recovering the chemicals used in the process, and of destroying the harmful oxygen-consuming wastes. McCain Foods in Florenceville have installed a $600,000 plant for the primary treatment of their effluent. A $1-million plant has been built into the new St. Anne-Nackawic Pulp and Paper Company at Nackawic. Woodstock has a $175,000 sewage treament plant in operation. And a $4.1-million sewage treatment plant is being constructed for the combined communities of Fredericton, Nashwaaksis, Marysville and Barker's Point. The Town of Oromocto and Base Gagetown had the foresight to install an elaborate sewage treatment plant when the community was constructed. Plans to install treat-

Editorial by John Braddock, *Atlantic Advocate*, September, 1969.

ment plants in other communities are going ahead.

For instance, the City of Dartmouth in Nova Scotia has spent $35,000 on a study for anti-pollution measures. The City of St. John's, Newfoundland, has spent about $36,000 on a domestic water supply treatment plant although, like other communities close to the sea, little has been done to treat the effluent before discharge. Other examples could be cited.

But the point is this: the Atlantic Provinces have a tremendous advantage over other parts of Canada and the United States: they are still comparatively unpopulated, and the industrial regions in relation to the total area are still low. We have the rare opportunity of installing adequate anti-pollution measures before the situation gets out of hand.

Expensive as we may think our anti-pollution plants may be, the cost is nothing compared to the bills faced by other regions of Canada and the States. Montrealers are scratching their heads and their pockets over the need to install a $131-million treatment plant. The communities around the Great Lakes look onto waters that each day are becoming more and more thick with algae, oil and slime. The Americans have estimated it will cost them over a billion dollars to clean their southern shores alone. Lake Michigan is considered in a critical condition. And so is Lake Okanagan in British Columbia, while nearby Skaha Lake is so polluted that back in 1967 it was found that people who swam there became ill. The Fraser River is polluted badly. A special committee is being set up to see to what extent the pollutants are sweeping down onto the Vancouver beaches. The Government of British Columbia is faced with a $12-billion bill if it is to set up a complete anti-pollution treatment program. The cost

may be higher, but it is not out of line.

Soon, perhaps sooner than we realize, we will all have to pay. Dr. Glenn T. Seaborg, chairman of the United States Atomic Energy Commission, recently stated that all twenty-two river systems in the United States will be biologically dead by the end of the century if pollution continues at the present rate.

Even more alarming is the effect of pollution of the sea, Dr. J. M. Anderson, head of the Fisheries Research Board of Canada Biological Station in St. Andrews, New Brunswick, is conducing personal research into the effects of DDT. He has discovered that a microscopic amount of DDT will affect a fish's learning process. What damage is caused in the way of migration and feeding and survival can only be guessed at, but it is well known that traces of DDT have been found from pole to pole, that the chemical has permeated almost every known species and form of life. Most horrifying of all is the real danger that could occur when indiscriminate dumping of chemicals into the oceans kills off microscopic vegetations found in the sea. It is now thought that this vegetation, through photosynthesis like land vegetation, contributes about seventy percent of our oxygen. Our careless habits could stifle ourselves to death.

The individual can take an active part to prevent pollution. He can keep his own surroundings clean. He can be careful of his own disposals. He can encourage, and be prepared to pay for, sewage treatment systems. He can demand that a percentage of his provincial tax be spent on anti-pollution measures. And, through public opinion and his Member of Parliament, he can persuade the federal government to carry out those anti-pollution programs that need national administration.

There is not a moment to lose.

THE GREAT CLEANUP
and what it's going to cost us

Leonard Bertin

Everyone appreciates sparkling water and clear blue skies, and most people prefer peace and quiet to the roar of city traffic and the scream of high-powered jets. The question that remains still to be answered is: How much are we prepared to pay for these rapidly vanishing luxuries?

A professor from Texas told a meeting in Toronto recently: 'There's no clean air left in North America. The only clean water you'll find is in the laboratory.' To some extent, what the professor asserted about today's conditions would have been equally true of the situation a hundred, a thousand, or even 10 million years ago. No air is truly pure. It always contains the breakdown products of vegetable decay and, very often, it is sullied with the dust of desert storms or forest fires, sea salt and debris from outer space. Even the whitest snow may have picked up some of this muck on its way down and, sooner or later, as the same water wends its way across and through the earth on its way to the sea, it will pick up elements and salts of all sorts from the ground and become 'hard'. But it wasn't contaminants of this sort, the result of natural processes, that the professor was talking about. It was those that are man-made, that have turned crystal clear trout streams into turgid

sewers and have occasionally even made the air over some of our cities foul to breathe and hurtful to the eyes.

Environmental pollution is many things to many people. Recently, it was defined by the U.S. Presidential Scientific Advisory Committee as 'the unfavorable alteration of our surroundings, wholly or largely as a by-product of man's actions, through direct or indirect effects or changes in energy patterns, radiation levels, chemical or physical constitution and abundance of organisms.' Of the air, it has been said that pollution occurs 'when wastes are produced so rapidly or when they accumulate to such concentrations that the normal self-cleansing properties of the atmosphere cannot cope with them.'

Rivers, too, have their own self-cleansing properties. The trouble is that, as man multiplies and covers the earth, and as his activities intensify, these natural potentials are completely overwhelmed. At this point, if someone doesn't step in and do something to remedy the situation and bring it under control, others are bound to suffer for there is only so much air, so much water, in the world. We depend on being able to use both these essential commodities, over and over again.

Dr. Albert E. Berry of the Canadian Institute of Pollution Control points

Reprinted with permission of *The Imperial Oil Review,* December, 1968.

out that, in our modern world, it must be accepted that the environment will never be entirely free of pollutants or other unnatural conditions. The air cannot be maintained free of all obnoxious ingredients, nor can water be the same as it was in the period before man inhabited the earth.

'It would be foolhardy,' he says, 'to think that conditions can be restored to that level. Neither is it necessary to do so. There is a level of tolerance below which man's well-being is not adversely affected. These levels have been prescribed over the years and are constantly subject to change. But no longer can it be expected that the environment will be maintained, even at this tolerance level, without involving expenditures and efforts.'

Man, went on Dr. Berry, must be prepared to pay out economic premiums because air and water are not as pure as they were originally. This must be considered as the cost of pollution brought on by man's activities. The main objective should be to see that the defined tolerance limits are not exceeded.

W. T. Perks of the National Capital Commission in Ottawa made a similar point. 'Although the "natural condition" is useful as a theoretical basis of measurement, it is virtually useless as an ideal for environmental improvement,' he said. 'Yet it persists in the ideology of pollution reform. We are constantly exhorted to "restore rivers to their natural condition" and to "prevent the atmosphere from being used for any kind of waste disposal". The costs of the ideal are frequently overshadowed by the moral force of the proposition.' But, if restoring the elements of the environment to their pristine state is an extreme goal, accepting the unmitigated pollution of air, water and soil is equally extreme, he says.

Two incidents in widely separated areas of Canada recently underlined the complexities of the problem. In Centreville, N.B., the citizens, normally a law-abiding lot, reached the limits of personal endurance one day last summer. The stench of rotting vegetation and dead fish in the Presquile River that flows through the city from the state of Maine got so bad they requisitioned five bulldozers and dammed the stream at the frontier. Said one housewife: 'We can't even try to live with that smell . . .' The pollution from a factory on the Maine side that process potatoes and sugar beets was such that a merchant said he feared the decaying matter could give rise to an epidemic. 'We've had the odor before,' he said, 'but it's never been that bad.'

Centreville is a case where, partly because of international boundaries, local authorities had been powerless to act. In Brantford, Ont., on the other hand, where the Ontario Water Resources Commission took a strong line and gave a long-established glue factory till Aug. 31 to do something about its pollution, the company responded by giving notice to 70 of its 100 employees. The president of the company said it would cost $300,000 to build and $50,000 a year to operate a waste treatment plant that would comply with regulations. With this financial burden to bear, the company's glue prices would no longer be competitive. 'The company has been doing business in Canada since 1896,' he said. 'If there was anything else we could do we would have done it.'

Dr. O. M. Solandt, chancellor of the University of Toronto and chairman of the Science Council of Canada, points out that, although the broad choices that have to be made are obvious in a general sort of way, they are hard to define precisely because they involve complex value judgments. 'I guess the first thing to be considered,' he says, 'is what we consider to be a tolerable level of pollution of any particular kind in a specified place, and what we are prepared to pay to avoid overstepping that level. Each decision reached interacts widely throughout our environment. Nonetheless, the problem must be faced and all available data assembled, analyzed and studied before a choice is made. All the necessary facts will rarely be available but it is better to use all the information that is at hand than to make blindly intuitive judgments.'

In a few cases, clearly definable tolerance levels of pollution can be set. Unfortunately, in many other cases, this is a value judgment based on complex and little-understood factors. An automobile graveyard, for example, may be necessary if the streets are not to be cluttered with abandoned cars, but to some people it represents an intolerable blot on the landscape. Acceptable purity of water means two quite different things to an industry struggling for survival and a fisherman out for sport.

'When it comes to deciding how much we are willing to pay for avoiding pollution or even for adding to the non-essential amenities of life, we are again in an area of complex value judgments, but also one where Canada is subject to some external constraints over which we have very little control,' says Dr. Solandt. 'There is probably no other country in the world that appears at first glance to have as wide a spectrum of economic choices available to it. At one extreme, we could follow the early pattern of the post-revolution Russian economy and put all available resources into productive investment to expand our primary and secondary industries. Our stores would contain only the bare necessities and most of the amenities of life would be absent, but our rate of economic growth would be

very high. At the other extreme, we could devote all of our very substantial earnings to the perfection of the welfare state and to investment in such admirable projects as parks, concert halls, museums and art galleries. This might be a very pleasant society but, with a dwindling source of revenue from productive industry, the idyll would not last very long.'

While it's obvious that neither of these two extremes would be acceptable to the average Canadian, it is not so obvious where the correct balance can be struck between investment in productive industry and longer-term social projects such as better education, better health services and highly desirable amenities of life like a pleasant environment. In making the best choice we can, says Solandt, we must recognize that Canada does not live in isolation, nor does the Canadian environment stop at the border. We are part of the world economy of nations. As such, we depend very much on exports for maintaining our high standard of living, and to maintain our prosperity we must remain competitive.

The predicament we are in is well illustrated by the pulp and paper industry which by the nature of its processes is a very heavy user of water and a major contributor to the biological death of many rivers and lakes. A single kraft (sulphate) pulp mill producing 1,000 tons daily may give rise to wastes equivalent to the sewage produced by a city of 200,000 people; a sulphite mill's waste may be equivalent to the sewage of a city many times larger.

Yet we cannot ban the pulp and paper industry, any more than we can dispense with electric generating stations or the petrochemical industry. The pulp and paper industry now comprises some 60 companies, which operate about 130 mills in nine of the country's 10 provinces and produce about $2 billion worth of goods a year, or nearly five percent of the gross national product. Nor can we, by the stroke of a new regulation, suddenly place on the industry restrictions so far-reaching that it would be uneconomic for them to continue in business in competition with companies based elsewhere. This is not to say that nothing has been done.

Quebec's 62 pulp and paper mills have spent $30 million in the past nine years to reduce solid wastes in their effluent fluids by about 2,000 tons a day. The remaining solid waste, however, is still substantial at 6,000 tons daily. The mills are working on further reductions of 860 tons a day to meet a December, 1969, objective they have worked out with the Quebec Water Resources Board. After hitting that target, the Quebec mills face a new directive for further reductions in the next five years costing an additional $80 to $100 million.

The pulp and paper industry's experience demonstrates one of the depressing aspects of pollution control — that costs go up far faster than improvements do. For example, during the five years from 1960 through 1964, the mills in Ontario reduced the solids in their effluents by 371 tons a day at a capital cost of $9 million. By the beginning of 1968 the amount of solids removed had been increased to 637 tons a day — nearly twice as much — but the capital cost had gone to $26.4 million — nearly three times as much.

For all Canadian pulp and paper mills to install primary and secondary waste water treatment, the Canadian Pulp and Paper Association's W. F. Fell and H. D. Paavila estimate the total capital cost would exceed $250 million, plus annual operating costs of $40 million. 'Yet even these measures would not assure compliance with the most stringent features of some present regulations,' they point out. Closing the last inch of that gap, says a CCPA spokesman, is simply not economically feasible with the present state of industry technology. The proper course clearly lies in concerted action, taken after proper discussion between industry and all levels of government, after all the facts have been ascertained.

Basically, much of pollution can be traced to conversion of vegetable matter or fossil fuels into energy or new products. Consequently, much of the opportunity for improvement lies in designing and manufacturing apparatus that will remove pollution at the source and convert it into useful energy or worthwhile products.

With industry expanding at the rate it has done over the last 100 years, the fact that pollution has not become completely intolerable is itself evidence of the work that has already been done by many companies to cope with the problem. Over the past 10 years alone, Imperial Oil, for example, has spent more than $40 million on facilities and measures that help to reduce pollution. Imperial's tanker fleet has done far more than was required by regulations to protect rivers and harbors; the 110,-000-ton *Imperial Ottawa,* the latest supertanker, features a sewage control system comprising septic tanks, sterilizers, combustion equipment and garbage grinder. Ontario Hydro since 1949 has spent $30 million on measures to reduce air pollution, and in some areas has achieved spectacular success. The large Lakeview station, for example, just west of Toronto, burns an average of 100 tons of coal an hour in each of its four units. In theory, each ton of fuel burned would result in the discharge of 200 pounds of fly ash into the atmosphere. In fact, only one pound gets out. The rest is trapped by electrostatic precipitators that now remove 99.5 per cent of all the ash produced.

When the Ontario Water Resources Commission in January, 1965, announced new objectives for the pulp and paper industry, the response of the industry was to appoint immediately a committee of three men, made available by their respective companies, to see what could be done. The committee visited all 42 mills in the province. Its findings showed that, in the period 1960-64, the total quantity of solids released into rivers had been cut by 255,-000 tons a year, at a cost of $18.3 million. Since then the mills have made further reductions of 271,000 tons — including estimates for 1968 — at an additional cost of $24 million.

The demand for further action by all segments of industry is widespread, to the point where pollution control has become a major political issue. In the last Canadian federal election, for example, anti-pollution legislation was a major plank in the platform of the Progressive Conservative Party and a survey of those who attended the Liberal leadership convention showed that delegates ranked pollution control just behind the constitution as a matter of national concern.

That this concern is shared by the leaders of industry is obvious from many recent statements. But all segments of industry that have inquired into the matter stress the need for action based on full consideration of all the facts. Precipitate action, taken hastily on the basis of insufficient information, could, it is emphasized, do incalculable harm to Canada's economic position without achieving the desired results. This is the stand taken by businessmen who must operate industries in compliance with regulations, but it is not their only stand on the question of environmental conservation. J. E. Baugh, vice president of Petrofina Canada Ltd., told a national conference on pollution in Banff earlier this year: 'The industrial community must accept pollution control as a mandatory part of doing business and cooperate with and assist government in setting acceptable standards and by operating in such a way as to remain within those standards.' Baugh went on: 'Canada sorely needs a strong cooperative program between the various levels of government and industry to establish national pollution standards. I believe the appropriate federal government department should aggressively promote further action with the provinces to undertake this project.'

The public, for its own part, must realize that progress cannot be achieved without enormous expenditures of money. Even the minimum cost in U.S. government budget studies is $2.5 billion annually through 1972 — and this does not include sewage facilities. Other studies call for $5 to $10 billion annually through the year 2000 to assure the availability of clean air and water in the United States. In Canada, one government estimate is $350 to $600 million annually through 1980. A study by the American Petroleum Institute came up with an increased cost of two cents per gallon plus a capital expenditure of four billion dollars in refining equipment to make lead-free motor gasoline.

Heavier fuels with low sulphur content will certainly add to our heating and hydro bills. These costs will inevitably be borne by the public, in higher taxes to pay for the public services and in higher prices to pay for the increased costs of manufacturing. How much we can afford to pay will determine the quality of our environment.

Six months and nearly a billion dollars later,

ADVERTISING OWNS ECOLOGY

Jerry Mander

Jerry Mander is president of Freeman, Mander & Gossage Advertising in San Francisco, a director of Friends of the Earth and author of The Great International Paper Airplane Book.

A few months ago, my partner and I were treated to a meeting with an experienced advertising man, about to open a new agency. His idea was to run a full-page newspaper ad (which he has since done) announcing that right from the first day, his office was going to devote 20 percent of its total time to "good" causes. He was going to raise money to fund this agency on that basis, and would I like to invest in this wonderful thing?

I asked him how he decided that 20 percent was exactly the right amount of time to give to saving the world, instead of, say, 16 percent or 28 percent. I don't think he got what I was driving at because he didn't leave, so I let it drop, but the point was that he was using "do-goodism" as a gimmick to raise money for an otherwise normal advertising agency and that whatever he did, do-goodwise, was bound to be phony.

It shouldn't have surprised me, really, because advertising people in general have an inordinate fascination with "image." They assume that by *seeming* a certain way, the world will come flocking around, tearing at their clothes. My late partner, Howard Gossage, used to say he preferred the word "identity" to "image" — the former having to do with the way one *really* is — which made him a lonely man in the advertising business.

Well, at one time, the difference may not have been all that important except for the psychic good health of advertising people and those few people whose idea of fun is to spend their day reading collections of ads. But the way I perceive it right now, at this point in history, the difference may be more like life and death.

Industry saves environment

With the sudden, immense outpouring of words from business and industry during the last six months concerning all the wonderful things they are doing to solve the pollution problem — most of these words being expressed in ads — its worth having a look at what's being said; of course, when seen close up, it's all image and no identity.

Most of industry still sees pollution and environment questions as more of a public relations and advertising problem — in other words, an image problem — than as anything fundamentally related to the way they are

Reprinted with permission of *Scanlon's Monthly*, June, 1970.

doing business. Shell Oil Company, for example, recently ran a four-ad series showing: 1) how they saved the lives of a lot fish by *not* polluting things as much as they had been; 2) how they are feeding starving millions by producing more and better pesticides (which on the other hand are killing the fish they just saved); 3) how they overcame a lovely little Connecticut town's fears that their new gas station would prove a blight because it would replace a number of lovely trees, by showing the townspeople that the station would itself be a lovely gas station, and 4) how they were against littering.

I'm sure that the president of that company feels that this position makes him a conservationist, because until recently it was unusual for an oil company even to mention pollution or ugliness. Now that there's public goodwill in conservation, now that it's a hot topic, it's "good business to think of the environmental *implications* of industrial action," as a major chemical company executive recently suggested.

Another example: a recent copy of the New York Times carried a Pan American Airways ad which announced "the latest breakthrough" in relieving airport congestion. I was ready to be told they had reduced their total number of flights, or scrapped the Boeing 747, or cancelled their SST orders. But it turned out that what they had done was to build a second terminal at Kennedy Airport in New York, so they could handle up to twice as many passengers with less congestion — inside. Getting the planes onto the ground without bumping each other is another matter, and getting passengers into New York City from the airport was somebody else's problem.

And we've all seen more than our share of power company ads. Usually they bring us one — or more — of four urgent messages: 1) use more

electricity; 2) the folks at your neighborhood power company are working like crazy developing new and creative means for winning the War on Pollution. (A recent headline from Pacific Gas & Electric: "We Put A Smile On Mother Nature's Face."); 3) we need more power plants to fill our growing power needs, atomic ones; they're as safe as chocolate ice cream; 4) they need a rate increase to finance the research.

I had thought I had already reached the pinnacle of my own shame and disgust concerning utility advertising — what are they doing advertising at all if they are a *public* utility — when by chance I came across an old congressional record and found a speech by Senator Lee Metcalf which somehow has gone unnoticed by the press and by conservationists.

Senator Metcalf pointed out that during 1969, public utilities spent nearly $300 million on advertising, *more than eight times* what they spend on research, all the while proclaiming in *the ads* their feats of anti-pollution research. Metcalf also noted that about a fourth of all the power companies in this country actually did no research at all, yet they spent millions in advertising to *talk* about research and to sell us all on using more electrical power at the same time as they tell us there's a power shortage. If advertising dollars are going to be spent by utilities, one would think — considering this so-called power shortage which makes the introduction of nuclear plants "inevitable," in the words of Newsweek — that the ads would be appeals to use *less* power.

It's also worth noting that like other utility industries, power companies work on a cost plus basis. That is, they add up all their costs and then they can charge you and me, say, 7.5 percent of the total and that's their profit. Advertising is included among the allowable costs and so you see they actually make more money by running more ads and artificially building up their costs.

The joys of nuclear power

Westinghouse Corporation has *really* jumped onto the ecological bandwagon. As one of the major suppliers of the technology needed to build nuclear power plants, Westinghouse has been running four-color ads everywhere, extolling the anti-polluting virtues of atomic power. The picture shows a beautiful girl sunbathing upon a lake which has one of those dome-shaped neo-modernistic nuclear plants in view. "Nuclear power plants are good neighbors," says the ad, "reliable, low-cost . . . neat, clean, safe."

And in a corporate brochure called "The Infinite Energy," we read about the pollution problems of conventional power systems and the marvelous advance that nuclear power represents. As for fears of radiation hazard, those are overstated, says Westinghouse. Even the sun, after all, produces radiation! "Sunshine is a gold blanket of radiation," reports the brochure. "The sun is actually a giant nuclear furnace operating much like a nuclear power reactor that is used to generate electricity. Overexposure to some of these rays is dangerous, just as overexposure to the sun's rays can be dangerous."

Simply ignored are the extreme dangers of "nuclear excursion" — of which there have already been several fortunately minor instances. A "nuclear excursion" is a leak in a reactor which could potentially cause the radiation effects equal to an atomic explosion, without any of the visual appeal. All buildings and inanimate objects within range would remain; only people and other living things would be done in.

The likelihood of such a disaster is great enough that Dr. David Lilienthal — a former director of the AEC — when asked his opinion of a proposed nuclear power plant in Queens said, "I wouldn't live in Queens if there was going to be a nuclear power plant there." And Dr. Edward Teller — no trainee in nuclear physics, and no bird watcher either — has said, "A single major mishap in a nuclear reactor could cause extreme damage, not because of the explosive force but because of the radioactive contamination. . . . So far we have been extremely lucky. . . . But with the spread of industrialization, with the greater number of simians monkeying around with things that they do not completely understand, sooner or later a fool will prove greater than the proof even in a foolproof system."

Westinghouse doesn't include *that* point of view while telling us of its concern with the environment. Nor does it, or any power company, while extolling the virtues of nuclear power, mention the radiation danger involved in the disposal of radioactive wastes. Nor do they mention that nuclear power plants produce another spectacular kind of pollution which is, if anything, *more* dangerous to the natural system than radiation, and that is thermal pollution: the water will be heated to the point where the ecological cycle will be disrupted, some species of fish or other living organisms will be killed, and whatever depends upon them for sustenance may not survive and so on up the line.

So much for Westinghouse's "nonpolluting" power system.

"Plant a lawn in a deep freeze"

Atlantic Richfield diverts us from their destructive Alaska Pipeline project by telling us that they are planning to seed the tundra areas done in by the pipeline. The fact is, they are going to *try* to plant grass, but no botanist outside the company thinks it's likely to work. And anyway, is planting grass a suitable solution for the terrible disturbances which the pipeline will cause to a very fragile wilderness?

Potlatch Corporation, a lumber company whose slogan is "the forests where innovations grow," has taken to running ads with pictures of trees and birds and rivers to show us that, as lumbermen, they have an intimate feel for the natural order. So while they are cutting down the innovations, we ought not to worry; they know what they are doing.

Coca-Cola ads tell us that it does offer "deposit and return" bottles but, on behalf of its customers who "demand" the no-deposit-no-return version of the bottle, they are continuing to put out that kind too. But just don't litter, they say, and everything will be all right.

Advertising is destroying the word "ecology" and perhaps all understanding of the concept. A few weeks ago, PG&E ran a headline advocating "a balance between ecology and energy." But ecology is not a thing that is balanced against anything else. The word describes a science of the interrelatedness of *everything*. Energy is a detail which only Man has decided to make a fuss over. That is what must be remembered, and it is getting increasingly hard to do so with this immense outpouring of diversionary, false and deadening information.

A billion dollars of reassurance

I am prepared to make the case that the $300 million in advertising spent by power companies (which, by the way, is about a third of the entire federal anti-pollution budget in Mr. Nixon's budget message), combined with the millions spent by oil companies, chemical companies, auto companies, industrial associations, the newly burgeoning anti-pollution industries, and so on — nearly a billion dollars, I would guess — is actually producing a net *loss* in this so-called War on Pollution. It's called cooptation in other circles, and I believe that it's operative here, perhaps not deliberately, but nevertheless.

All of the government rhetoric, magnified by industrial assurances, has the effect of destroying the power of the ecology message. People's eyes are already beginning to glaze at the sight of still more jargon about saving the world. It's awfully hard to out-shout roughly a billion dollars of advertising money. Especially when you consider that last year's total offsetting advertising expenditures by for-real conservation organizations were only roughly $200,000 — or two-hundredths of one percent of the industry output.

The net effect of all this media spending and the government's cultivated image of activity is to encourage a society already dazzled by technology to be further assured that technology is solving the problem — people want so much to be assured — and so it's back to the television set. Perhaps even worse than the fact that the ads are misleading — even lying in many instances — is the fact that they divert the reader from a more basic understanding of what's really going on: that technological society is beginning to reach its limits, economic expansionism is going to end, and endless consumption is going to end, and we're all of us going to begin adopting some of the techniques of peoples who live on islands, say, and for whom a finite system such as island Earth, is a given.

If we don't develop that understanding of the limits of things, of the islandness of Earth, of the fact that we are wildlife, too, then all the anti-pollution messages and money will be useless. Suppose our technology does manage to develop a pollution-free car engine? Will *that* make it acceptable to cover the landscape with highways and automobiles?

Advertising a dying industry

A short while ago I made some of these remarks to the San Francisco Association of Industrial Advertisers. I even went so far as to tell them that I personally believe advertising is a dying industry. Tied as it is to an expanding economy and given that we live in a finite system, on an island in space, advertising is doomed, eventually, at least in the form we now know it. If you don't need to sell more of a thing, then you probably don't need advertising.

If advertising has any future at all after, say, the next ten years, it will probably be more in the area of propagandizing for issues of one sort or another, basically issues which help expand the individual rather than the economy; or perhaps we'll have advertising of products that are related to issues — such as for a company which really has found a way to harness the sun's energy as a clean power fuel; or, it will be purely informational in nature: "We have eight old Fords here today."

I had expected, frankly, to be attacked by this industrial group — for having attacked them and for the nonsense about a no-growth economic system which didn't include advertising the annual style change. Instead, the response, after the first few minutes, was giggling, chattering under the breath and staring at the ceiling. Nobody was the slightest bit upset. Nobody *was listening.*

It was a very depressing evening. I eventually went out and got drunk with a Wall Street Journal reporter interested in the implications of the no-growth system. He had seen the no-response and remarked that for the first time, he really believed the world *was* coming to an end.

Business and advertising and public relations have gotten so adroit at imitating honesty that many of us have gotten out of the habit of just leveling, taking the good with the bad and hoping that since the basic intentions are good, things will work out. We can't avoid trying to steer the world back in our own direction. So the truly gratuitous act rarely takes place. Yet I believe a San Francisco dressmaker, Alvin Duskin, could be elected mayor of San Francisco with a little bit of effort, and it's only because he gratuitously committed himself publicly on a subject of concern — not turning over Alcatraz to H. L. Hunt — and at the end, he didn't try to sell anyone dresses, or finish up his stand with some catchy slogan like, "Always Interested in Beauty, Whether on Ladies' Dresses or in Your Bay."

But that kind of gratuitous behavior is very rare indeed. It is, in fact, discouraged as being unjustified by profits, whereas ads which self-serve while seeming to be taking up controversial questions in the public interest, are given extreme praise for their image of involvement.

For example, the most prestigious of all advertising awards are those given annually by Saturday Review "for distinguished advertising in the public interest." But what *they* call "public interest" is not exactly what you'd call public interest. Here is the way Saturday Review defined the way to think about the award-winning ads:

"Although corporate advertising does not have as its primary objective the direct sale of specific products to the consumer, it certainly does create and maintain a favorable selling climate among customers and prospects. It skillfully cultivates the image of quality. . . . Insofar as a corporation communicates a feeling of company responsibility, good neighborliness, and an awareness of public service, the sort of campaigns submitted in SR's 1970 competition must pay off not only in community relationships where the company operates but among its citizen customers."

It should therefore not be very surprising that this year, out of 40 awards, 16 (40 percent) went to power companies, oil companies, chemical companies and mining and extracting companies, all of whom have a lot of "good neighborliness" needs to get across. Only three awards went to what you could call "do-good" institutions, if you are prepared to think of the American Institute of Architects, Blue Shield, and the Advertising Council as "do-good" institutions which are something beyond sophisticated lobbies. (Howard Gossage once said of the Advertising Council that it was willing to advocate causes, "but only those that would be thought of as controversial by people who are for cancer or against safe driving.")

As for Saturday Review's "18-Year Honor Roll" of award winners, it shows 20 winners, 11 of which are companies engaged in extracting — Weyerhaeuser, Shell Oil, etc. — and three of which are chemical companies in need of communicating "a feeling of company responsibility, good neighborliness and an awareness of public service."

Human chauvinism

Whereas corporate "institutional" advertising used to show pictures of labor and capital shaking hands, now it's "business and ecologists working together to control the environment," as a bank ad recently put it. Technology will take care of everything. Man's ingenuity will win out. Even the Ford Foundation says so.

I recently approached Ford about a project which had the possibility of countering the glut of industrial eco-advertising: an advertising foundation, funded by Ford and managed by a coalition of militant though "respectable" conservation groups. The ad foundation would be manned by the literally hundreds of ad men who have made known (to me, and also publicly) their interest in working solely on this subject — even at half salary. They would create ads which reveal the half-truths and omissions in industry ads; fight on specific issues as they come along; and undertake to educate the public as to truly basic, not cosmetic, solutions to the environmental crisis. They would take up such questions as life-styles, consumption patterns, the need for a no-growth economy in a finite system, the requirement that technological innovation ought to be scrutinized from the point of view that it is guilty until proven innocent, not vice versa.

It didn't take long for this Ford man, a certain Mr. Felling, to dismiss the project as hopelessly naive and to go on describing Ford's work in teaching young children how to "better manage the environment." The meeting broke up when I told him that that sort of education — "managing the environment" — would do far more harm than good. We are already *managing* the environment, and that's why we are in the mess we are in; it is a further example, borrowing from Women's Lib, of what let's call *Human* Chauvinism.

It hardly matters whether one believes that we were given dominion over other living things or we just took it, but in any event our excuse is that we've got the brains and can use machines, giving us some kind of de facto royalty status. As a result, however, we have removed ourselves from the processes that formed all the other living things; we forget that the fabric is all connected and we are just a thread of it.

Every ad that espouses a new technological intrusion into natural systems, even as a solution to pollution, encourages us to forget that fooling with one stitch alters the whole fabric.

Controls on advertising

We already see many signs that what began with cigarette advertising is likely to become the model for all advertising within industries which drastically affect the environment. Cigarette advertising, after all, is demonstrably less of a menace to society's survival than the advertising of pesticides or detergents or lumber or power.

Friends of the Earth, in concert with other conservation groups, has begun proceedings to apply the results of the Fairness Doctrine case against cigarette advertising to advertising of polluting industries. If they succeed, as I believe they eventually will, all radio and television stations will be required to provide a conservation organization with time in which they may present a counter message to an ad. If an automobile company runs a one-minute spot advertising its new model, Friends of the Earth could indicate what the implications of the annual style change are. Or they could talk about the pollution from cars, or the raw materials that go into building them, or the problem of disposing of them. And the roads needed to run them on. When a Standard Oil ad for its F-310 appears, calling it "the most long-awaited gasoline development in history," they will be able to put it in perspective by showing that the gas represents only a five percent pollution improvement, leaving 95 percent, and that the ad is filled with deliberately misleading information.

So far, I'm afraid, that sort of government interference strikes me as the only way to mitigate the effects of the millions of ad dollars which are being spent to tell just one side of the story. The only other alternative is for ad people to get on the firing line and influence what kind of message is going down. It might be that a new period of laying it on the line would then ensue and we'd all be better off.

Advertising people are, by and large, intelligent; it's a question of commitment. I hope that more and more find themselves in the position of Mr. James Webb Young, who retired himself from the business one day to work for some worthy foundation. When asked why he did it, he said, "One morning I woke up and I didn't give a damn whether they sold more Quaker Oats than I sold Cream of Wheat."

WHO WILL FOOT THE CLEANUP BILL?

To economists, America's current ecological crisis comes from ignoring the deceptively simple fact that the gross national product has a mirror image: gross national pollution. As the nation's production and consumption of goods has soared, so has the size of its various wastebaskets and the costs involved in emptying them. "It would not be surprising if these costs were in the tens of billions of dollars annually," says Allen V. Kneese of Resources for the Future, Inc., probably the nation's leading expert on the economies of pollution.

Rising concern for the quality of the environment and very real evidence that many regions have reached a dangerous upper limit for pollution will mean that, in the future, a large share of the cost of waste disposal will have to be borne directly. Not only will the out-of-pocket costs be high, but the process of solving the problem might work some far-reaching changes in the principles of the American free enterprise system.

Doctrines. This week, while scientists in Boston were discussing the technological aspects of pollution control, economists attending the annual meeting of the American Economic Assn. in New York were speculating in their own jargon-filled ways about the economic aspects of it.

There were two centers around which the debate formed: a paper on "Externalities and Public Policy" by Harvard University's Kenneth J. Arrow, a mathematically inclined theorist who rates high in the economics profession; and another entitled "Economics as a System of Belief" by former New Frontiersman John K. Galbraith, another Harvard economist whose popular following makes up for the support he lacks among economists.

Each, in his own characteristic style touched on what has become the central tenet of the economic analysis of pollution: that widespread ecological damage is evidence of a widespread difference between the "private costs" of economic decisions (reflected in monetary prices) and their "social costs," which include the impact on the environment.

For those trained in the tradition of Adam Smith, the divergence of private and social costs is of major ideological significance. Classical economic theory holds that, through the operation of the price system, the free market automatically allocates resources to their socially most efficient uses. But some markets, such as those served by public utilities cannot be free. Traditionally, this has been the strongest argument for government regulation. Now, the price system is seen to be defective

Reprinted with permission of *Business Week,* January 3, 1970.

when it deals with environmental factors. And this is becoming a justification for intervention in what had been private economic decisions.

Converging. This was the basic premise of Arrow's discussion of the significance of "externalities," such as the effects of pollution. He proved by mathematical formulations that society would be better off if it developed some "nonmarket mechanisms" for allocating resources where private costs and social costs were substantially different. His presentation was too arcane for most of his audience, which dwindled from several hundred to less than 50 in the course of the lecture. But Galbraith made the same point in unmistakably direct language as he delivered an attack on the traditional concept of "consumer sovereignty."

"Consumer sovereignty makes pollution and other environmental disharmony an external diseconomy," Galbraith said. "The cost of damage to air, water, and surroundings is borne by the community, not the producer. Since the market is assumed to be an efficient expression of public taste and need, external diseconomies have been [considered] of peripheral significance to be corrected by essentially cosmetic public action."

Actually, Galbraith argues, it is not the consumer who is sovereign but the producer. "Environmental damage becomes a normal consequence of the conflict between the goals of the producing firm" (which wants to engage in the unhampered pursuit of productive efficiency) and the public, he insists.

Few economists would go so far as Galbraith in advocating "the replacement of the sovereign producer with the sovereign state" in determining society's pattern of consumption. But many are coming to the conclusion that the ecological crisis will be solved only when the cost of potential harm to the

environment is included directly in the cost of various products. The result, of course, would be a significantly slower rate of real growth over the next generation, at least as growth is currently measured.

Hardening. From this perspective, economists are coming to argue against the carrot and for the stick in the campaign against environmental pollution. Direct financial incentives (such as Congress' recent action in maintaining the investment credit for pollution control devices) will not do the job, the argument runs.

For one thing, they subsidize activities that contribute most to pollution. For another, unless they cover almost the entire cost of abatement efforts, they still leave companies with the difficult decision of how much profit to sacrifice for the public good. And they offer no inducement to managers to find more efficient ways to eliminate pollution.

Another tactic may be employed. Stiff antipollution standards may be set, forcing major polluters to "internalize" costs that are now borne by the public at large. But, as Allen Kneese sees it, "these standards would become a part of the natural impediments to business enterprise." Managers would try to find the most efficient means of meeting the standards and, to the extent that they were unsuccessful, the cost of waste disposal would get built into product prices, thus discouraging the use of products that contribute significantly to environmental damage.

Corporate managers, of course, can hardly be expected to be greatly interested in theorists who would solve ecological problems by making a manager's job more difficult. But what looks on the surface like pretty woolly theorizing is already being translated directly into a program with considerable political appeal.

Last month, Senator William Proxmire (D-Wis.), with the support of nine colleagues, introduced a bill that would levy a federal "effluency fee" of 10¢ per lb. for industrial wastes emitted into the nation's rivers. Citing Kneese as the main inspiration for the idea, Proxmire estimated that the system would produce about $2-billion a year, half of which would be used to subsidize municipal waste treatment.

The annual cost of pollution control

[Billions of dollars]

	Capital	Operating	Total
Air pollution:			
Automobile afterburners	$1.5	$1.0	$2.5
Sulfur dioxide removal from stack gases	0.3	1.0	1.3
Industrial control equipment	0.3	—	0.3
Total	2.1	2.0	4.1
Water pollution:			
Reservoirs for seasonal equalization of river flows for waste oxidation	0.4	—	0.4
Municipal sewage collection and treatment	0.9	0.6	1.5
Industrial effluent treatment	1.1	0.5	1.6
Separation of combined sewers and storage of storm waters	0.5	—	0.5
Electric utility cooling towers	0.1	0.6	0.7
Total	3.0	1.7	4.7
Solid waste disposal:			
Collection of municipal wastes	—	2.6	2.6
Incineration of municipal wastes	—	0.7	0.7
Land fill of municipal wastes	—	0.3	0.3
Junk auto disposal	—	0.2	0.2
Demolition waste disposal	—	0.9	0.9
Total	—	4.7	4.7
Total	**5.1**	**8.4**	**13.5**

Data: Harvard Center for Population Studies

24/100

SCIENCE YELLS FOR INDUSTRY'S HELP AGAINST POLLUTION

The U.S. will be saved from strangling in its own waste only if there is a total upheaval in public attitude, only if industry gives as much thought to getting rid of outworn products as it did to producing them. Armed with their present knowledge, scientists may stall off the worst. But, in their eyes, the pollution of the U.S. has gone far beyond the point where technology alone can stop it.

This was the bleak warning spelled out at this week's 136th annual meeting of the American Assn. for the Advancement of Science, attended by more than 7,000 scientists in Boston. "There's only one solution: the reuse and recycling of everything," summed up the AAAS's incoming president, oceanographer Dr. Athelstan Spilhaus. "To get this rolling in the next five years will cost at least $50-billion [in subsidies to industry and increased production costs]. That's a guess, but also a minimum."

Musts. Spilhaus and other top scientists listed the most urgent needs:
- Using available technology, a number of stopgap remedies must be applied to cut back existing pollution.
- Industry must take over, from public agencies, a much heavier burden of waste disposal.
- The public must be educated to recognize the mounting danger, to prepare for the approval of heavy public

and private spending to fight pollution.

Dr. S. Fred Singer, deputy assistant secretary of Interior, detailed just what the U.S. is up against. Every year its people and industry spew out 360-million tons of garbage, 1.5-billion tons of solid waste from mines and factories 142-million tons of air pollutants and over 50-billion gal. of polluted water. Heat from power plants flows into U.S. streams and air; noise is mounting and 2-billion tons of sediment a year wash off U.S. farms, laden with water-polluting chemicals.

Each American contributes 32 tons of solid waste a year and an estimated 135 gal. of sewage a day. And worse is to come. Says Singer: "Environmental quality goes down as the level and affluence of the population rises."

Weapons at hand. Only a fraction of this outpouring is adequately handled today. Municipalities, for example, collect only half the garbage their people create. But the technology exists now to reduce many woes of pollution.

Air pollution, about 60 percent of it caused by automobiles, is a prime target for immediate technological attack. Scientists expect that, by 1980, improved fuels and control devices will cut the amount of auto emissions by one-third, to 60-million tons a year. But it will probably increase again, to 70-million by the year 2000, as the number of registered vehicles more

Reprinted with permission of *Business Week,* January 3, 1970.

115

SCIENCE YELLS FOR INDUSTRY'S HELP AGAINST POLLUTION

The U.S. will be saved from strangling in its own waste only if there is a total upheaval in public attitude, only if industry gives as much thought to getting rid of outworn products as it did to producing them. Armed with their present knowledge, scientists may stall off the worst. But, in their eyes, the pollution of the U.S. has gone far beyond the point where technology alone can stop it.

This was the bleak warning spelled out at this week's 136th annual meeting of the American Assn. for the Advancement of Science, attended by more than 7,000 scientists in Boston. "There's only one solution: the reuse and recycling of everything," summed up the AAAS's incoming president, oceanographer Dr. Athelstan Spilhaus. "To get this rolling in the next five years will cost at least $50-billion [in subsidies to industry and increased production costs]. That's a guess, but also a minimum."

Musts. Spilhaus and other top scientists listed the most urgent needs:
- Using available technology, a number of stopgap remedies must be applied to cut back existing pollution.
- Industry must take over, from public agencies, a much heavier burden of waste disposal.
- The public must be educated to recognize the mounting danger, to prepare for the approval of heavy public and private spending to fight pollution.

Dr. S. Fred Singer, deputy assistant secretary of Interior, detailed just what the U.S. is up against. Every year its people and industry spew out 360-million tons of garbage, 1.5-billion tons of solid waste from mines and factories 142-million tons of air pollutants and over 50-billion gal. of polluted water. Heat from power plants flows into U.S. streams and air; noise is mounting and 2-billion tons of sediment a year wash off U.S. farms, laden with water-polluting chemicals.

Each American contributes 32 tons of solid waste a year and an estimated 135 gal. of sewage a day. And worse is to come. Says Singer: "Environmental quality goes down as the level and affluence of the population rises."

Weapons at hand. Only a fraction of this outpouring is adequately handled today. Municipalities, for example, collect only half the garbage their people create. But the technology exists now to reduce many woes of pollution.

Air pollution, about 60 percent of it caused by automobiles, is a prime target for immediate technological attack. Scientists expect that, by 1980, improved fuels and control devices will cut the amount of auto emissions by one-third, to 60-million tons a year. But it will probably increase again, to 70-million by the year 2000, as the number of registered vehicles more

Reprinted with permission of *Business Week*, January 3, 1970.

than doubles from today's 100-million. From 1975 to 1990, the public will probably spend between $96-billion and $141-billion on auto maintenance and control devices. But if the number of vehicles grows as expected, this spending will not change the quality of U.S. air. Such estimates will spur current demands for a substitute to replace the internal combustion engine.

Assault on sulfur. Meanwhile, a potentially far-reaching assault has started on sulfur dioxide, one of the worst air pollutants, largely produced by coal-burning power stations. A new technique called "fluidized bed" combustion is under test in Britain and Pennsylvania, the AAAS was told by Dr. Arthur M. Squires, professor of chemical engineering at New York's City College.

The method, by which the fuel floats on a cushion of air blasted from beneath it, promises to cut power production costs, allow recovery of commercially salable sulfur, and largely eliminate coal-fuel sulfur pollution, says Squires. Moreover, it may be able to permit burning up of mine tailings, such as the millions of tons of waste now disfiguring the Pennsylvania countryside.

Even by the year 2000, oil- and coal-burning power plants will still make half of U.S. power output and there will be more of them than today. But nuclear reactors are a big, new factor moving up to limit further additions to industrial air pollution.

The reactors have powerful friends. Says Dr. Chauncey Starr, dean of engineering at the University of California at Los Angeles: "Nuclear reactors are going to be the saviors of the power industry in terms of clean air."

But they also have critics. Squires, for instance, denounces them as "primitive machines" because, he says, they consume irreplaceable uranium

that will be needed in about 20 years as "seed corn" for breeder reactors, which will make much more efficient use of uranium fuel.

Thermal threat. But nuclear power reactors are mainly under attack because they cause thermal pollution, ranked by scientists as a definite threat to U.S. waterways and lakes. Of all the water that is used by U.S. industry for cooling, about 80 percent is used by power-generating plants, and each nuclear plant churns out about 40 percent more waste heat than a fossil-fueled power plant.

To curb the thermal threat, scientists at the AAAS meeting urged the dispersion of all new power plants of every type to prevent concentration of heat outflow. Another strong likelihood is that more power plants will be built on coasts so that waste heat can be discharged into the ocean.

A far greater threat to U.S. water resources is an old, familiar one: city sewage. And this is one area where science is advanced enough to provide treatment techniques for any desired degree of purification, if money can be found to finance the effort. At Windhoek, in the parched, South African highlands, "complete reuse of waste is practiced," reports Singer. He estimates that, to obtain such a result from a three-stage treatment plant, it costs 30¢ to 40¢ per 1,000 gal. However, two-stage techniques that are potentially quicker and cheaper are already in the pilot-plant phase.

Pressure on industry. Industry, however, dumps about three times as much organic pollution into U.S. waters as do the 120-million people served by sewers. And there is a rising cry by scientists that industry, and not public agencies, should clean it up. The concept of levying charges on environment polluters is supported by AAAS past president Dr. Walter Orr Roberts, who sees these charges as both deterrent and a source of public funds to mop up existing pollution.

Another form of pollution which scientists insist can be slashed using current knowledge is noise, which medical experts told the AAAS may cause damage to human nerves, blood vessels, and even unborn babies. They nervously await the sonic boom effects of the supersonic transport and note the doubling of noise levels around some airports in the past decade.

Elsewhere the level is rising steadily, too. Increased street traffic has raised city noise levels by one decibel a year for the past 35 years. Anti-noise laws must be passed, says acoustics expert Dr. G. J. Thiessen of the National Research Council of Canada, to govern the machine user and to ensure that no manufacturer of noisy machines gains a price advantage by leaving silencing devices off his products.

Grappling with the problem of solid waste, scientists suggest that industries producing this kind of waste should reclaim it, especially the packaging and auto industries. Packaging contribute about 35-million tons a year to the nation's refuse, or about 20 percent of it. This includes cartons, paper wrappers, 25-billion glass bottles and jars, and 50-billion metal cans.

The auto makers' contribution is about 7-million cars junked every year. But some day the auto industry may find itself compelled to design cars that, when junked, can be "recycled" and completely reabsorbed into the industry as raw materials. "Various positive and negative tax incentives could be used to accelerate the educational process," says Singer.

In fact, there is urgent need for every industry, and not just the auto industry, to recycle its products, says AAAS President-elect Spilhaus. The government should subsidize the changeover until companies can make a profit under a recycled system, he thinks. "It's a funny thing to suggest — subsidizing the junk business," Spilhaus notes, "but I feel we must."